# THE OWL

*The trials and tribulations of a Radio Ham and a DX-er*

By

Lee Marsland

**RB**

Rossendale Books

Published by Lulu Enterprises Inc.
3101 Hillsborough Street
Suite 210
Raleigh, NC 27607-5436
United States of America

Published in paperback 2017
Category: Life Story/Memoirs
Copyright Lee Marsland © 2017
ISBN : 978-1-326-94674-6

All rights reserved, Copyright under Berne Copyright Convention and Pan American Convention. No part of this book may be reproduced, stored in a retrieval system, or transmitted in any form or by any means, electronic, mechanical, photocopying, recording or otherwise, without prior permission of the author. The author's moral rights have been asserted.

## Acknowledgements

There are a number of people I would like to thank and acknowledge for their help in making this book a reality. First is my long-suffering wife Val, her help, understanding and not least her purse, which has been instrumental to my being in this hobby for so long. To Ron, G4DIY for help on our adventures, and as a source for some of the photographs. To my Grandchildren Dan and Amy. I hope I live a little longer to stop you selling my equipment! To my sons, Lee and Barry, for their help. To Alan G4NXG for stepping up when needed. Also, thank you to Tate for the sketches and Amy for going through the images. Thank you also to Ron M0COC, Steve G0KXL, Brian G4WSE and Paul G0WRE for the photos.

*For all the people who for whatever reason, decide to read this journal, and expect to see perfect grammar and spelling, then let me apologise in advance.*

*I have decided to try and compose a record of my incredible amount of "cock ups" related to amateur radio. I am not normally accident prone, but then, there is no such thing as a perfect first time installation, no matter how 'little' forward planning goes into it!*

## Contents

1. How It All Started ................................................... 9
2. Up, Up and Away .................................................. 17
3. An Aerial Goes Aerial ........................................... 26
4. And They're Off! .................................................... 31
5. Problems With the Neighbours ...................... 37
6. Purple Rain ............................................................. 45
7. The Owl is OK .......................................................... 58
8. Another Tower Tale ............................................. 69
9. Talking Stateside ................................................... 74
10. Happy Harry ....................................................... 102
11. Caravan and Other Sites ............................. 130
12. Family Matters .................................................. 142
13. The Channel Islands ...................................... 156
14. For Ron, Alan & Lee Junior ........................... 170
15. Reflections ......................................................... 174
Glossary .................................................................... 176

## 1. How It All Started

For as long as I can remember I was always going to be a "DXer" and try to work all those exotic countries around the world. Then, after getting my results after taking the Radio Amateur Examination in December 1984, I applied for and received the call-sign G1MEF. I must admit this is not the most inspiring of call-signs, but as a good friend Harry G4GHS told me the phonetics could be, Middle East Forces. This was far better than MEF, which in my area is a derogatory name to be called.

Thanks to my very good friend and Morse mentor, Tony Bailey G4XSN who helped and put up with my frequent visits to teach me CW during weekends. Tony would let me under his supervision work some wonderful DX from his station. Tony would call CQ or answer a CQ call and after he exchanged his report he would then ask them to listen for me. All the stations worked were really pleased to get a G1 prefix into their log, as it was quite a rare prefix in the early eighties, and got us into some very exciting pileups.

Tony G4XSN

Tony lived in Anfield which is very close to the city. His home was at the end of a very long street of terraced houses. His aerial was a TB3 made by Jaybeam a manufacturer in the Midlands. It was on top of two scaffold tubes and was guyed all over the place. His radio was a brand-new Kenwood TS 830S and he had the Yaesu FL-2100Z. This was a high-end station that I could only dream of owning. I vowed that when I got my Class A licence that this was the way I wanted to go, and be a "DXer." With good radios and the best antenna I can get. I will never forget Tony's philosophy on aerials which was "the bigger the cow pat, the more flies you attract." I truly believe that never have truer words of wisdom been uttered by a mortal man!

After just over four weeks of visits to Tony's house, I was ready in his opinion for the dreaded CW exam. In the Liverpool and District Radio Society, of which I was a member, there is a name that when mentioned could make grown men tremble, well Class B licence holders about to take the Morse exam that is. A name akin to the boogey man called Mr Jardine. Mr Jardine was the gentleman who took most of the Morse proficiency tests in Liverpool. All the Class A licence holders in our local club used to wind up the lads going for the CW test, and it was a well-known fact that Mr Jardine did not suffer fools lightly. You were certainly in for a tongue lashing if he thought you were not ready or too nervous to complete the test and therefore wasting his time. According to club members, he was about fifteen feet tall, weighed about eighty stone, a square shaped Scotsman who did not like Scousers! Especially the ones that could not read his twelve words per minute CW!

So I telephoned the centre in Liverpool, and was told that the next available appointment for the Morse test would be in two months time. Such was the demand by new licence holders in the early eighties, that people were travelling from all over the Northwest to take their CW test and the waiting list was vast. Still, I was not going to allow this to stop me reaching my goal and becoming a hallowed "DXer."

I found out you could take the telegraphy test at a coastal radio station. After a little phoning around I found just the place, Nebo.

Nebo was a telegraph station on the Island of Anglesey in Wales. When I phoned the station, I was told I could take the test in four days time! I can remember the days leading up to this event. I was bricking it! I did not want to let my friend down after all his hard work, nor did I want to blow my chance of being a 'DXer' not to mention the fee for the exam!

On the morning of the exam I set off with my mentor Tony and a fellow ham Eddie G0AUD. I recall arriving on the island and having just crossed the bridge over the Menai straits, we called into the "Little Theft" or sorry "Chef" for breakfast. I was assured that a good breakfast would make the exam a lot easier. Although in hindsight, I later thought I'd been conned as I paid for all the meals!!

On arriving at the telegraph station at Nebo, I recall two Welsh lads coming out of the station. They were really looking miffed that they had both failed. Tony in a boost of confidence building remarked that after eating a breakfast like we'd had, I couldn't possibly fail.

As I introduced myself to the examiner, whose name I never got, I was told that he conducted the test by playing a tape with the exam on it. I remember him asking me where about in Liverpool I was from, and him telling me he was originally from Bootle which was about half a mile from my QTH. Then he asked the million-pound question. "What team do you support?" Quick as a flash I replied "I only supported my wife and children, but if I were to follow football then it would be the same as him!" Good answer as it seemed to pacify him as "On to the test" he said. He told me that he would play a sample of the test, and if I could get it all then he would play the whole test. If I struggled with it he said he would not cash my cheque for a week and I could come back re-sit it, wow, what a nice guy! He then said "but if you struggle and think that you can get it by chance, and you fail, the cheque will be cashed and you would not get a refund." Apparently that option was taken up by the two previous Welsh lads, and they failed.

After listening to the test tape I found I was getting every character, and then he suddenly stopped it and said, "You will have no problem." He then restarted the tape and I was taking the exam, on my way to the golden ticket. It came to my sending skills next "You're not going to adjust my key are you?" "No." I replied. I recall just after sending the first characters, him asking me to "Slow down." He told me that there was no hurry, unaware I was sending about twenty-five words per minute. Next came the numbers, then half way through the test he said, "Come and see my motorbike." I was confused and asked "Did I pass?" he replied "Yep" and went on to show me his pride and joy a Honda 50cc motorcycle painted in Everton blue and white colours, including decals. "Fantastic" I said, I was on about my test result, but he thought I meant his pride and joy, the motor cycle! That's how I passed the Morse test, and got my class 'A' licence, and around April 1985 I became the proud owner of G0DBE, "Dog Biscuit Eater."

*Anglesey Radio Station Nebo*

## 2. Up, Up and Away

Armed with my new call sign I bought my very first second hand HF radio, a Trio (Kenwood) TS-120V,TL120L 100 Watt Linear, PS30, AT120 ATU and finally the SP120 speaker completed the station. All this for the princely sum of £450 from Bob, G3PDC.

At this time propagation was very good on 10 metres, so I decided after spending all my cash on the 120 line-up, I would build (homebrew) my first HF Antenna. After much thought I decided on quad, constructed using carpet canes and multi-stranded copper wire. Not only would it be a cheap build, but in my eyes, it would be a real thing of beauty.

I only had a very light weight Hirschman TV rotator to turn this magnificent beast with its two elements. The Hirschman Rotator was placed on top of two scaffolding tubes at 30 feet. T and K brackets secured it to the wall and some nylon clothes line to guyed it off safely. Or so I thought!

Let me explain my shack. I called it my shack but my young son called it his bedroom. I recall my arguments with him about my radio equipment and the subsequent risk of death if he played with it, but still that did not stop him popping a screwdriver into the vent at the rear of the power supply, and toasting it along with my liner! I managed to replace outputs on the power supply, but the linear was just too damaged for me to repair, so I was forced to operate QRP. That was inconvenient as 10 Watts made it a challenge when wanting to break a pile-up. I purchased a very heavy duty lorry battery for going out mobile, and operating from the local beach. With an ex Mod tank whip I found that my low power DXing was really enhanced by operating near the shore near salt water.

*"My shack." "No my bedroom!"*

So on to the antenna - the quad - what a brilliant piece of work. I was working Australia and Japan in the morning and the United States in the afternoon and evening. About three weeks into my groove of being a "DXer" I became aware that the band was prone to sudden changes. Whilst I was talking to a station in VK (Australia) I started to notice deep QSB on the signal I was receiving, then suddenly, the signal would build up again. Nothing unusual you might think, but other stations local to me were not experiencing the same phenomenon. Then, one evening talking to the States, I noticed the station I was talking to was 5x9 then 3x3 then 5x9 then again 3x3 again. This was just not right and I was wondering what was going on with the ionosphere, then suddenly, my radio started to move towards the window! I stared at it for moment and it was then I thought someone was stealing my coax!

I ran down the stairs, grabbed one of the kid's rounder's bats ready to tackle any nasty yob trying to make off with my coax/antenna. When I entered the back garden, I was confused as no one was there! Checking the garden and rear entry I saw nothing out there. I was completely at a loss. It was then I shone a torch at the scaffolding which was still in-situ as were the guy ropes.

I then realised it was a little more windy than usual. Looking up I could see the quad spinning around and around. It seems that Hirschman TV Rotators do not like quads, and the quad had eaten it. Swinging side to side, it just shredded all the gears, and this accounted for the unusual QSB! Finally, it gave up spectacularly when the wind had blown the thing around and around wrapping the coax around the scaffolding which resulted in the coax pulling the radio towards the window!

I ran upstairs to find the PL259 plug straining at the window frame and it was starting to pull the frame from the wall! First plan of action was to cut the coax. Out I went to the car to get the tool box, (note to self, keep tools in house in future) Retrieve cutters, run back upstairs and cut the coax. In the meantime, the window frame is now about two inches' outwards from the bedroom wall – snip – job done!

I decided I would sort the problem out right away by trying to secure the antenna to stop it spinning around like a helicopter rotor blade. I grabbed the coax that was hanging down outside the window and pulled it trying to unravel the cable. Around and around it went and finally it was free, but how to stop it swinging around again? This was now the next challenge. After all, the DX was calling and I needed a quick fix right now to get me back on the air. Then it was like someone flicked a switch, I knew what was needed!

Being a keen sea fisher man I had the answer in my tackle box. I got my fishing reel that was loaded with thirty-pound breaking strain mono-filament line. If I could get this through the loop of the quad I could manually pull the antenna into the direction I wished to talk, and stop the aerial from spinning around and pulling the coax around the poles again. All I needed was a decent weight to tie the line to and then hay presto a temporary rotator!

Looking through the fishing tackle box I found a six-ounce lead weight. This was more than heavy enough to throw through the loop and take the line through. I took careful aim at the gap in the loop and threw the weight. It sailed through the loop like a dream, but then I realised I had been a little enthusiastic in the strength of my effort to get the lead weight up there. It flew like an Exocet missile through the loop, then continued over the roof and off it went into the night! I distinctly heard it land on the other side of the house and into the street beyond. I then thought 'Oh my God, my car' so I then ran through the house and was about to open the door, it was then I heard shouting and screaming coming from outside. To my surprise the ice-cream man had just pulled up to sell his goods when my line complete with lead came whistling over the roof. I feel I should point out that opposite my house is a telephone pole, and the lines fan out from this pole to most of the houses on both sides of the road. The lead weight went over the roof and over the telephone wire that came from the pole to my next-door neighbour's house. As the weight went over the wire it started to drop towards the floor, but followed the line in the direction of my neighbour's house. Unfortunately, the ice-cream man had parked outside my neighbour's house and right in the path of the travelling lead weight!

The noise I had heard was the weight hitting and smashing the window on the side of the van. Thinking caution might be the best option I did what every other person in this position would do. I peered through the letter box. I must stress that this decision wasn't an act of self-preservation, but I thought discretion the best policy in a situation like this!  Anyway, that aside, looking through the letter box, I observed the ice-cream man shouting and cursing at none existing kids whom he had assumed threw the object that broke his window. I then thought if he went near the window he might see the weight dangling from the fishing line and therefore he wouldn't need Sherlock Holmes to track it to my roof! So I ran back into the garden and pulled the line back up hoping to get the evidence away from the scene.

Not thinking about our friend Isaac Newton and his theory of gravity, once the weight was clear of the ice-cream van it continued its merry way along the telephone wire and it connected with my neighbour's house, well the window really! I continued pulling the line and managed to get the offending object out of sight. Thank God it was dark. The weight came back over the roof and I had successfully snagged the loop. I tied it off before I went back through the house to the front door. As I was about to open it, I could hear the shouting and arguing, my neighbour was out in the street fighting with the ice-cream man. My neighbour had thought the ice-cream man was responsible for breaking his window and vice-versa. At this stage I thought it would only get more confusing if I were to own up, so playing the good neighbour I invested my time breaking them apart. Now I know you are thinking what a baddy I am, but it turned out the ice-cream man was guilty later of supplying more than ice-cream to his customers and that lessened my guilt.

*"Stop me and buy one"*

## 3. An Aerial Goes Aerial

The quad proved to be a very good antenna, and I was steadily racking up my country score, but the maintenance was overwhelming. I had used stranded copper wire for the elements but this stretched and the resonant frequency would consequently lower, so I changed the elements to hard drawn copper. This proved to be a little better as it did not stretch as much, but it proved to be brittle and with the elements flexing in the wind it would break on the corners due to fatigue. The best material was stainless steel MiG-welding wire. I had to use silver solder and a small gas blowlamp to make a good connection for the feeder, but it worked. About a month later a storm broke three spreaders so it at that stage I decided that although the quad was an exceptional antenna, it was to high maintenance. Time to move on!

Timing could not have been better, as Jaybeam TB3 with a Diawa rotator became available and was just what I needed to replace the quad. I purchased the beam and invested in some new lightweight aluminium scaffolding tubes to raise the beam up. The tubes were twenty-two feet long and with the two feet long stub mast it would raise the beam up to about forty-three feet with the rotator in place. This was to prove my most ambitious yet! I bought three K brackets and Rawl bolts, fastened them to the wall of my house, then to 'belt and brace' the project I put guying brackets on the pole and bought new rope. No wind was going to bring this bad boy down!

On the morning of this great installation, I readied my helpers which consisted of one neighbour, one brother-in-law, and one XYL. Thinking carefully about what was going to happen, the plan was to connect the tubes and then place the bottom of the pole at the wall of the house and my neighbour would then foot the base of the pole. The other end would be over the top of the fence at the end of the garden. I would bolt on the rotator and the stub mast then bolt on the beam with the help of my brother-in-law. My XYL would pass the tools and coax etc, and make the coffee. Good plan.

Everything went together and it looked the part while resting on the fence but now to get it vertical next to the house and next to the T and K brackets. I went over the plan again. My brother-in-law and I would walk the pole up while my neighbour would foot the bottom to prevent the pole kicking out. My XYL would then pass me the u-bolt and would then fasten the said pole to the K bracket. What could possibly go wrong?

Off we went, My brother-in-law and I started to walking from the beam end pushing up, but the further we went towards the house it was not lifting the beam off the fence. There was just a giant bow in the tube. Slowly the beam rose, but as it did the beam started to swing and was in danger of the elements being bent if they hit the floor. My neighbour seeing a disaster unfolding decided to un-foot the base. He then ran to the beam and before I could say anything he gave it a huge push!

Well things went very hairy from that moment and the beam took on a life of its own. It shot skywards like a two-bob rocket, it pulled out of my hands and for a split second it was vertical. It was about the same time I noticed that no one was footing the base of the pole! The beam continued its way. With the combined weight of the rotator and beam, plus the flexibility of the poles, it took it over the roof. In fact it pole vaulted over the roof and when the base went out from the wall it somersaulted over house as well! It went across the road and although this happened in a spit second it seemed to be in slow motion.

I can remember the shouting, the noise, and the look of disbelief on the wife's face all in the space of a milli-gilli-zilli second. I was dreading what awaited me at the front of the house. Do you remember those bloody telephone wires from my previous story? Well no need to worry about them now! The pole had gone across my garden, over the road, and lay across my neighbours drive opposite. It took out all the telephone lines, but miraculously it missed both my neighbour's car and mine! As for the beam, well it broke the reflector off, bent the director and boom, and cracked the clamps on the stub mast. It was at this point that both my neighbour and brother in law said "Goodbye" and left me to it. Luckily no one got hurt and the only damage was to the beam and the six telephone lines. Thankfully I had Tony my cousin who worked for British Telecom and he bailed me out of the proverbial. Eventually I settled for twenty-five feet of pole and got the repaired TB 3 up successfully.

## 4. And They're Off!

Needless to say, I did not advertise the fact that I was just a little accident prone, and whilst sitting in our local radio club with a few friends and fellow amateurs, one told me he wanted to install a telescopic tower at the rear of his house. He was looking for some volunteers to help with the project. Given this would be a first-class opportunity to learn how to install a tower and antenna I was among the first to offer my help.

I did not for one minute think it would turn out to be like the Krypton Factor, and it would be a labour of love digging a two-meter-deep hole in clay! Then after making the template to line up the bolts in the base plate, of which I had no input, Bill G0JID went to the builder's merchants to collect the materials for mixing the concrete, I think he brought enough to build a bypass! Have you ever seen the grit, stones, and cement to mix two cubic metres of concrete? It took about fifteen trips in Bill's old Proton to bring the bags of stuff to his home from the builder's yard.

Well, Bills friends started to disappear pretty quick, we were doing this marathon relay between the yard and his home. So much so, that when we had finished hand-balling the cement etc down the entry to the rear of his house, there was only three of us left! Did I forget to mention the bags had to be carried from the middle of a block of terrace houses around the top of the street, then down the entry to the third to last house from the bottom? When the last bag was deposited in the entry, Bill informed us he was off to the local tool hire to collect a cement mixer after leaving me with Alan, who was a sixty-year-old friend, to bring the bags in from the entry. Alan by the way it turns out was a good supervisor and was able to offer lots of words of wisdom and encouragement whilst leaving me to carry all the bags into the yard! Yes, yours truly was a pack horse, and I am proud to say that in the spirit of friendship I got all but three of the bags into the yard before Bill got back two and a half hours later. It was at this stage I must admit I told

Bill I was losing the will to live and that the final three bags were all his. I told him I was off home now, but promised to return tomorrow and give the job a good coat of looking at!

A promise is a promise and the next day I returned to Bill's house. I went around the back through the entry along which I had helped carry all the materials for Bill's hole. I was greeted by Bill and Alan, I was distinctly aware of the lack bodies to help mix the concrete. I could not help but notice there were only two spades! It was then that Alan told me he was on water duty. I must admit we managed to mix and pour the concrete; it only took us four and a half hours. True to his word Alan did a sterling job using the hose whilst Bill and I mixed and barrowed the concrete down the hole. It was a good job that Alan stopped with his advice when he did or he may indeed have become part of the project. Alan wished me to point out that in all fairness he did in fact make one brew whilst in charge of the water! With the template in place and the concrete poured, it was a High Five moment on a job well done. Even Alan was included.

While waiting for the concrete to cure, and the tower to be delivered, Bill said he may as well get the coax and rotator control cable into place. Bill explained that he was going to operate from the front room of his house, so the cables would have to go over the roof and down the front so he ended up drilling through the window frame and into the living room. Ah! I have been down this road before, remember the fishing weight? I was an old hand at this, and suggested throwing some string or rope tied to something from the front of the house. I asked Bill to find something suitable, but not something that could kill or harm someone if it went too far. I didn't want Bill to be in the situation I had been in. Bill looked around and I could see his attention drawn almost immediately to a large rubber dog bone! What possible harm could it do being made of rubber?

After tying a length of clothes line to the bone and the other length to the cables, I got Bill to take ownership of the throw. Well what can I say? It went off like clockwork; Bill produced a throw that would put Jeff Capes to shame. He launched it over the roof and there were no cries of pain or alarm. Well done Bill! Now all that was needed was for it to be pulled over the roof to where the tower was going to go and hey presto, all sorted!

Just as we finished tying the rope to the coax, the coax decided to take on a life of its own! Suddenly, it all started to go over the roof and pick up speed. I remember how bizarre Bill's face looked when it continued to fly over the roof so far that the end of the cables disappeared over the apex. Running through the house, to the back, we were just in time to see the cable go through the gate. We just got to the gate in time to witness Bill's dog disappearing down the entry, bone in mouth, towing the cables behind it!

To this day, I still remember that look on Bill's face as he chased the dog; the bone and the cable down the entry. Good plan though and successfully completed after the dog was later locked in the house. Two weeks later, the tower, antenna and rotator- complete with cables were installed. Job well done!

"And they're off!"

Over the years, Bill gave me a run for my money in the pileups. Then suddenly after returning home from the gym, Bill had a massive heart attack which sadly took him from us. He was only 46 years old and he is greatly missed.

## 5. Problems With the Neighbours

I had a lot of fun at my old address, I worked lots of DX and I enjoyed my time chasing US counties. I even gained my own Stateside QSL manager, Joe WA2PJI. I'm very grateful to Joe as he did literally handle thousands of QSL cards for me.

Joe WA2PJI

I was watching the television with the children when I heard a knock on the front door, I was greeted by a gentleman who with his identity card in his hand introduced himself as Mr Dobson, a DTI investigator, and was calling to identify me as a possible source of causing interference to a neighbour's television. He told me that no fee had been paid yet so they were just there to verify that I was in fact a Radio Amateur and not an operator on Citizen Band. Having no problems reported to me I was surprised by his presence, but as I do not own any illegal equipment, and I kept a very good log, I allowed him in. It must have been one of the only times my shack was really tidy. That and the fact it was my son's bedroom and his mum was always doing the house work up there, so up we went. Having made a list of the station details, Mr Dobson left and apologised for disturbing me. He told me It would be unlikely I would hear from him again as everything seemed in order.

Two weeks later I got the knock on the door, Mr Dobson was back. "The fee had been paid; I wonder if it would be possible do a test on your station?" I know that they are supposed to give a certain amount of notice, but I thought I would like to get a free check, and besides I did not know of any other local amateur having a signature in their log giving it a clear bill of health, so lets go for it!

It was then I discovered who had made the complaint, next door but one! Now in all fairness they had never told me, nor give me an opportunity to remedy any problem. Anyhow Mr Dobson's partner went into my neighbours, and Mr Dobson went upstairs with me to the station. The first thing he did was make sure that the station was still the same as when he had last visited. Then whilst in communication with his partner in the neighbour's house, he asked me to transmit without getting, or making a contact. It wasn't too long before his colleague contacted him and said that my neighbour's television was practically dancing around the living room!

I distinctly remember the look on the guy's face, and I thought that's it! I'm getting an enforcement order to close me down. He then told me he was going down to his car to bring in some measuring equipment. After a short meeting with his colleague Mr Dobson returned to the shack carrying a spectrum analyser. He connected the analyser to the last part of my equipment. Now by this time in my involvement with Amateur Radio, things had moved on slightly, I still used the Kenwood TS120V, but I had at this time bought a small solid state linear amplifier, the SL 250 DX, It was a 200 Watt broad band linear with a built in pre-amp. So the last thing in line before the antenna was a Kenwood low pass filter after the linear.

After connecting the analyser to the low pass filter via a patch lead, Mr Dobson asked me to whistle into the mic at full power! So I did as I was told and let out one long whistle until he yelled at me to stop. I can still hear that loud "crack" and come to think of it, I can still smell the acrid stench of expensive electrical components lingering in my nostrils! He didn't really need to tell me to stop as it was apparent something had failed in a spectacular way. I got a bad look off him when I said "I hope you haven't damaged my equipment!"

After a heated discussion, out of ear shot, Mr Dobson returned to the shack with another analyser, and brought with him the attenuator he should have installed earlier. With everything connected he told me to whistle once more, but with only ten Watts this time! Now I have never seen a spectrum analyser before, but even I could see a clean signal on the scope, then he brought up the first, second, and third harmonic signals. After the fundamental signal the scope showed a very small first harmonic and none on the second and third. So, he then told me to do the same on all the bands I operate on, again nothing. Things were looking good, and now for the real test, full power, two hundred Watts. Again, there were no spurious emissions from my equipment. This made sense as I pointed out to Mr Dobson; if there had been a problem with the station it would soon become apparent as there would have been a long queue of disgruntled neighbour's outside my door!

It turns out the neighbour had hired a Bush VHS video player from a store and it was very susceptible to outside transmissions, the preamp was overloaded with my RF and it was a simple case of swamping the signal. It turned out to be an easy fix with ferrite rings and a simple braid breaker. I would have done myself had I been told in the first place. Well all's well that ends well happy neighbours. My station given a clean bill of health, and my log signed to that effect by Mr Dobson on behalf of the DTI. Shame about the analyser though! After signing my log, Mr Dobson informed me my station was all clear, and should anybody knock on my door complaining then show them the signature and report in my log book. He followed it up by telling me to basically tell them to "p**s off!"

*Checked and tested, a clean bill of health.*

About a month went by and the same gentlemen, Mr Dobson come knocking on my door again! He explained that he had received a telephone call that the neighbour's TV was again receiving interference. So, remembering what he told me to say on his last visit, I told him to "p**s off!" "You don't tell me to do that" he replied, he seemed really upset at me; I can't think why I had only repeated his instructions. Well I allowed him in and he went upstairs and checked his notes to see if I had changed any equipment in my station, (which I hadn't) we went through the same test with his colleague in my neighbour's house. Using the analyser (with the attenuator in line!) he again gave my station got a full bill of health. It transpires that my neighbours husband had removed all the filters from the TV and Video recorder and thrown them away, so after replacing all the filters once again I was told he would be getting a bill for both sets of filters along with a call out fee! So, after a second test recorded in my log, I said goodbye. I couldn't help but ask him if I should tell the next person who knocked over interference to "p**s off." I won't even try to describe the look he gave me. Then after two station checks for spurious emissions by the DTI I moved to my current address.

## 6.  Purple Rain

I recall after about three days of my arrival in my new house, the housing manager came to see me. "Due to the material that the house is constructed from, you will not be allowed to fix or attach any pole or aerials to the house". To be honest, this was really a forgone conclusion, as my house was a prefabricated house (pre-fab built during World War Two to help with the housing crisis after Mr Hitler decided to re-arrange the landscape). The house had been modified during the mid-seventies and been cladded with aluminium sheets around the first floor well as the roof. We did not have rising damp; we had falling rust! And instead of a front door key, we had a tin opener! These were the pearls of wisdom from anyone who did not live in Tin Town.

Anyway, I asked the manager if he had any objection to me putting an aerial on a support mast, this being  installed away from the metal cladding. He told me he didn't care if it wasn't fastened to the house. Wow! To me that meant I could get a tower and that there would be no problems from my landlord. Little did he know that I would take advantage of his words.

Being just a little wiser than I was at my old address, I decided that I would go about it with the legal process and apply for planning permission.

First, I decided that I would lobby my neighbours and get them to sign a letter of consent. I did this for a couple of reasons:
 1. It would let me know if any of them would be likely to object to my application;
2. If they did then it would they give me an opportunity to speak to them and maybe talk them around?
3. I had an idea that if I got the neighbours to sign the letter of support, then the council would be unlikely not to send out letter of proposal.

Well anyway, it worked, and finally, understanding a little psychology on how people think, they are less likely to object after signing the support letter because they would not wish to appear two faced! Well, that was the plan anyway! I worded the letter so that it was clear and relevant to the planning issue. It went like this:

*I have been informed by Mr Lee Marsland that he intends to put a support mast at the rear of his house for the purpose of his hobby. Mr Marsland has fully explained the reason behind his application for planning and I wish to let the planning officer know that :*
*A. Having discussed the proposal, I have no objection to the said application*
*B. I object to the proposal and I do not support the application.*
*Signed*
*Printed*
*Dated*

Then off I went to all my neighbours, taking my six-year-old daughter with me. I thought they would be less likely to tell me to f*** off with her present!

To my surprise, every neighbour I visited signed and had no objections, wow! What a coup. I submitted the application to the planning office with the fee, plans for a sixty-feet tower for experimental purpose, and my letters of support. About three months later I had planning permission. I feel at this point I must point out that again things do not quite go to plan. My garden is not very large, and it soon became apparent that when I submitted the plans; I had not considered the space it would need to tilt it over. The tower when tilted only just fitted into the garden and that was without either the head unit (rotator housing), stub mast to fasten the beam to and of course the antenna.

It turns out that if I was going to be able fit this tower into the garden, and tilt it over, then it was going to have the base post in front of the kitchen window, that was the first hurdle, then, when it did tilt to install the antenna, I then have to rely on the generosity of my next-door neighbour! This would be the second hurdle!

The first Hurdle was soon overcome when my wife was going out on a shopping spree with family. I had all day to get the hole dug and the ground post installed. A quick telephone call to a good friend John G0IEW, and twenty minutes later John arrived. The ground post was twelve feet long, and out of those six feet was to be buried.

I marked the site where we going to place the base and we then started to dig. Things were really going well, unlike the ground at Bill's site, the soil was very loamy for about ten inches, and then the ground went to compacted sand. In next to no time we were down about three feet! Once we went past three feet the sand become wet, very wet, in fact the deeper it went the wetter it become.

Now if I was going to get the post in the ground before the wife got back, I'd need to arrange the concrete. Bearing in mind mobile phones were the size of house bricks, and the fact is I did not even own one. I left John to continue digging whilst I went to the local Spotmix to arrange delivery as soon as possible. With the time of arrival for the concrete sorted for three thirty in the afternoon, I went back home to finish off with John and let him know our schedule time. The first thing I noticed when I arrived was the size of the sand pyramid in my back yard! "Bloody Hell John, Where are you?" From down the hole he replied. "Down here" John was standing in the bottom of the hole! It was close to seven feet deep! Water was up to his knees, getting deeper! "The sides keep falling in" He exclaimed; I reached in and helped drag him out, it could have collapsed at any time! John told me later he was "so in the groove" He just carried on!

About an hour later Spotmix arrived, by then the water was about three foot deep! "Digging a well?" the Spotmix driver asked. This was going to take some serious concrete to fill the Bugger up I thought. I had got the ground post level and straight, it was braced with 3x3 inch wood to prevent it moving whilst the concrete was being poured. After eighteen barrows of concrete and still no sign of progress I began to think if John had made it to Australia! It was at this stage I started to throw in house bricks, paving slabs, the rockery. Bikes! Anything to start offsetting the amount of concrete!

Eventually after two and three quarter metres of concrete went into John's black hole, we finally finished. I cannot tell you how much it cost me because if the wife ever read this, I'm dead!
Within a month, the tower was installed and a Hy-gain TH-6 installed. The best thing about getting permission for experimental purpose is you are not restricted to what antenna is placed up in the air!

*The Hy-gain TH-6 DXX*

Well experiment I did! I took the TH-6 down and installed a five element Yagi for 10 metres. Then I tried a two element 3 band quad for 10, 15 and 20 metres. Fantastic antenna, but I wanted to go a little bit bigger. I made a six element quad on a sixty foot boom for 10, 15 and 20 metres. Boy what an antenna! I could work everything I could hear. Another plus note, high gain, low noise, full size, it increased my country score very quickly.

On the down side, 'BIG'. Living near the coast we get lots of wind, and maintenance was an issue. I have spoken to many people that have used quads over many years without any mishaps or maintenance. Unfortunately, this is not the case with mine. Two things made me change from a quad to a Yagi:
**Maintenance**.
As I said in a previous chapter, mine was up and down more times than a bride's drawers!
**Insomnia**!
You really don't sleep well with a large quad in a really strong westerly wind!

When they decide to fail, and take out your neighbour's green house and send your insurance policy up, then it's definitely time to think about Yagi!!

So, a Yagi it is, but which one can compete against a six-element quad? Easy. A six element Yagi. Being on a fifty-seven-feet boom, (three feet shorter than the quad) that should reassure the neighbours and the XYL! It was a thing of beauty, and made with a lot of love and effort. I made a six-element log cell Yagi on a fifty-seven-and-a-half-feet boom, and it used full size elements, all homebrew.

On the first morning after the build, I tried it out using a Kenwood TS-440 and a Heathkit SB-1000 linear. I can still hear that very first pile up from Oceania and Japan. I got on the air about 07:20 on 14.207 mhz, and after making sure the frequency was clear I gave a CQ call. Just like fishing you never know if your call was heard or where the reply will come from. I had a general idea, but like fishing you can be pleasantly surprised. Either way as a rule it's rare to get a bite first cast or in this case with the first

CQ call. Immediately a JA (Japenese} called me and what a signal, it truly was 5/9 +10 db. Over the course of the QSO(conversation), which we had for about seventeen minutes, I observed no QSB (fading signal) at all. As soon as I finished I called CQ again and it was then the band erupted, and I found myself in a fantastic pile up of JA, VK, and ZL. (Japan, Australia, New Zealand).

Two hours later and 76 QSO's in the log, I was pleased to say "it works". From that day on it was a similar story, North America, Pacific, in fact it was a little too easy. The real test was in a big pile up, one or two calls and you were in the log.

There was a down side to this phenomenal antenna. I was getting easily two to three hundred QSO's a day! This meant a lot of QSL cards to honour, and as a rule most JA sent a card for every QSO. It was becoming very quickly expensive, and I was going through QSL cards at an unbelievable rate. As it turned out this was not my main problem no, the biggest problem as it turns out was the XYL! A fifty-seven-foot boom and six elements make for one really big bird perch, not just in Litherland where my QTH is located, but the whole of Liverpool! There were hundreds of the buggers up there, and my wife was getting really hacked off re-washing the cloths she put on the washing line.

The thing about Starlings, whilst not being a big bird, they have a bum the size of a peanut, by the time it hits the floor from about seventy feet, it has expanded to the size of a saucer! Worse still is when they gorge out on Elder or Blackberries in the autumn, its then like purple rain! I wonder if the pop star Prince was a Ham. At times there could be over a hundred flying rats up on that antenna, so a solution had to be found.

Whilst talking to a range of Australian and Stateside Hams on the radio, it was clear that this was not just a problem in Liverpool but worldwide. I found lots of other amateurs had similar problems with various types of birds, and soon it become clear that lots of people had different opinions on how to solve the problem. Here are just a couple of examples of the suggestions proposed. "Shoot them!" Well that was a non-starter for a few reasons, what goes up must come down, and I do not think my neighbours would be too impressed with dead birds or lead shot raining down on them or their property. Not to mention the inevitable visits from the Police, RSPCA etc. Next put a buzzer or siren on the boom and frighten them. Again, consider the impact on the neighbours.

Try tying fishing line along both the boom and elements, logistically a nightmare and too difficult. A much cheaper and easier solution would be to smear grease all over the boom and elements. This would work for maybe a couple of months. The idea being the birds would fly up to the antenna, when it comes into land, because of the speed coming in the bird would attempt and grab the element which because of the grease it would spin around and around until it eventually hangs upside down like a bat and drops off! Downside of this idea is autumn, we get lots of balsam seeds from the trees locally which looks like cotton wool floating, in other words covering the antenna in a carpet to keep the little darlings feet warm in the winter!

So after much research I had the answer. I knew they used to use birds of prey to keep airfields clear, so a large bird of prey was the solution. The answer came from the local garden centre. An owl! Not just any owl, but an enormous plastic eagle owl.

*"The Owl"*

## 7. The Owl is OK

The saga of the owl, you know when I think back on this I know that people are going to think I have made this up. That it's a figment of my mind and fictitious, but I swear that it is the truth and really deserves a chapter of its own.

The birds really were becoming a nightmare. The house, conservatory, garden, pond, washing, everything was a target for those flying rats! But it was the size and shape of the bird do do on my car that was the final straw! I was convinced that a pterodactyl had dumped on it and I could take no more. "Purple Rain"

I had seen two fantastic, two-foot-tall eagle owls at the garden centre about a month earlier. I knew birds are afraid of birds of prey. So, it was a natural choice for the project. Hindsight is a good thing in these things and I am really pleased that there was only one owl left when I went to the garden centre. It was around two feet tall and was painted very realistic.

The other owl that was out of stock had wings that flapped when you tugged a string. Again, about two feet tall and knowing what I know now would probably have got me either divorced or locked up. Anyway, the owl I got was better than the heron I looked at and smaller.

After parting with twenty-five quid (owls don't go cheap) sorry, poor pun. I brought it home and two days later I installed it near the reflector. Luckily it had a one inch hole in the base and a hook moulded to allow you to, I presume anchor it in the garden. I used a small bracket and mounted the owl on a one inch piece of aluminium pole and cable tied it to the boom. I must say sitting up there at about seventy feet it looked really good. Test came the following morning. I went out and looked and behold success. No starlings, not one. I remember coming home from shopping, looking up, and I saw that there were three birds sitting on the director at the opposite end of the aerial.

By the third day, they were sitting on every element from the driven to the last director but still none on the reflector. It wasn't looking good, by the end of the week not only were they on the reflector but sitting on its head! In fact, I'm sure that one even had his wing around the bloody thing!

Then it happened, a knock on the door. I was busy working a pile up of State side stations when the wife came into the shack (The Dining Room) and informed me there was someone at the front door for me. I asked the station I was talking to, to stand by while I went to see who was interrupting my county hunting.

Standing on the door step was a young lady in uniform. I first thought it was a police officer, but then she informed me she was an RSPCA officer (inspector no less!) and she had come in response after being notified of a distressed owl on the aerial that had been reported as not moving for several days! Ok, I thought, this is a wind up, and my first thought was its Jeremy Beadle outside with a hidden TV camera. I thought he was about to pop up and try to make me look a fool on the television. Well! I was not going to be taken in, and I told her so. Boy was this girl a good actress, she kept a straight face all through the conversation, I would hate to face her in a game of poker!

The poor woman was trying to keep her composure and kept telling me how serious she was and was here because a letter and three telephone calls had been received about a distressed owl trapped on the pylon in my garden. It was at this point my patience run short "Distressed, Distressed" I sort of said a little aloud, "I think you would be bloody distressed if you had a two-foot tube shoved up your arse woman, its plastic!" At this point she just held up her id card and still with a straight face told she was a real RSPB officer and she was not trying to wind me up.

Glancing over her shoulder I could see the official RSPCA ambulance parked by my neighbours and that looked very authentic. It was then I heard the little voice in the back of my head telling me she might be for real. Oh, my God! What have I said? So I calmly explained my dilemma with the starlings. "Oh" she said like it was a call she made every day. "Man web normally inform us when they install decoy owls on their pylons so we can put the public's mind at rest if they call us reporting a bird trapped or in distress." I explained that it had nothing to do with Man web it's not a pylon, and it certainly wasn't a decoy as I was trying to get rid of the buggers.

She then came out with how the RSPCA had received a letter and three telephone calls regarding the owl and it looked real to the untrained eye. I explained the reason it looked real was to frighten them off, not give them something to cuddle up to. I then got her solution to help prevent them getting any more calls or letters "could you maybe put a sign in the window or in the garden to inform people it was not real".

To which I only had one reply, "No" "these are Scouse starlings and are very clever they would soon read the sign and they would then take up residence on the bloody thing close the gate on your way out!" I remember my wife's comment when I walked into the house, "I knew that bloody thing would cause us problems didn't I tell you" how prophetic and how annoying when later over the years she repeated "I told you so". That was the first of many incidents involving the famous plastic beast on Moss Lane. About two weeks after the dreaded knock, I received a letter from the RSPB. It went on to detail about the cruel way I'd trained the owl to perch on the antenna all day and night and it then went on to threaten me with prosecution. It also included a membership form to join the RSPB and was signed by H R Puffinstuff. The lads at my radio club were really getting good with their computer graphics, and as it was done on an old spectrum 64 it was very good. Even the headed paper looked Authentic. Well done lads!

Val my wife was about to go shopping when a gentleman walking his dog stopped at the gate "That's an eagle owl" he informed Val "they are really rare!" he went on. Val making sure that the gate was securely closed informed him that it was plastic. "Very intelligent are eagle owls" he told her. Again, she told him it was plastic "they are easy to train" he went on. "That's why your husband picked it above all other owls" By this time Val was backing up the path "Mind you" he said "Its really clever the way your husband has trained it to walk from one end to the other". At this stage, Val was back in the house ready to phone the police. "I told you it would cause trouble" said Val later.

It has become over the years a local landmark. Taxi drivers ask "Which end of the lane do you want, the end with the owl?"

One of the most bizarre days was when my friend Scotch Billy and I were doing some work on our boat on the drive. I kid you not this lovely blonde lady about twenty-five years old pulled up in her car outside. She came over to us and informed me she breeds Barn owls! I nearly asked her if it hurt, but quickly thought better not. I explained that it was an eagle owl and made of plastic, she didn't look like one of the usual nutters who drive past pointing and shouting at the owl to make it fly off. It turns out the lady was with a group of people trying to save our small local population of Barn owls and although she knew the bird was not real it still fascinated her. She then informed me that she teaches at the local primary school and would I object if she brought some of the pupils to observe (her words not mine) the owl. How could I refuse to agree anything from this stunning weird blonde lady! I said yes. Later that afternoon, a minibus pulled up onto my drive and ejected about fifteen young children. They then set up camp on the grass outside my house and started to draw pictures of the owl. Val the wife came out, saw them all and offered biscuits and orange juice! Talk about bizarre. They were there for about half an hour then just before they all packed up to go, the lovely blonde lady brought one of the children over who then presented me with a picture of my owl on the antenna including all the birds perched up there! What can I say?

I have named but a few of the weird and crazy things people have done and said and there are many more like them, but there is also a down side to installing the useless plastic object up there.

I was talking to a good friend on the radio when I heard a screech of brakes from outside the house. Being close to a school I immediately went to the front to see what was going on. To my horror there was a cyclist lying on the grass verge. It was clear to see he was badly injured and had been knocked off his bike by a car. It turns out that the cyclist was passing by my house, and the driver of the car was too busy looking at the owl. Not noticing the cyclist, he collided with him knocking him onto the grass verge. The bike was really buckled and bent so I knew the guy was in a bad way. When I got to him I could see he was in a lot of pain and shivering, so I went back inside upstairs and grabbed the duvet off the bed to put on him. The wife's favourite duvet I might add. After putting it on him I left him in the care of others while the ambulance arrived, so I went back on the radio to tell my friend what was going on outside. He was asking lots of questions and I was trying my best to answer them. When I went back outside to see what was happening the cyclist had gone and so did the wife's duvet. How do I explain this one to her? Then those words rang in my head I told you that bloody thing would cause us problems.

*The Owl in action!*

That's it, its coming down, a week later I brought it down, I hardly recognised it! Apart from it being bleached and brittle from ultra violet rays it had been the target for every delinquent local with an air rifle. There were that many lead pellets in it I could have weighed it in at the scrap metal yard!

So much for conserving local eagle owls! Then the following day it started. "Where's the owl?" everyone passing, including people in cars would stop and ask where it was, I couldn't believe it. I gave up after about three months I installed another, just to keep people happy! Even when it's not up there the bloody thing caused problems.

## 8. Another Tower Tale

Over the years, I have met a lot of people who have remained friends throughout Amateur Radio I would like to think that I am not the only Amateur that has encountered "slight hiccups" when engaging in the hobby. I will not name the people who like me made monumental booboos, but I was involved with a ham who after listening to my QSO with another local ham whilst he was sitting on the toilet! I kid you not. He claimed that he enjoyed the QSO so much; he felt the need to introduce himself to me.

Although the gentleman was originally from Liverpool, he moved away to a town not too far away, but far enough to become a "plastic Scouser" (and an Evertonian to boot!). I met him on 10 metres in the mid-nineties and we had regular QSO's (daily). He was often mobile with his work commitments, but no matter where about he was in the country, I worked him. Scotland, Wales even down south. Our furthest QSO was when he was on holiday in Antigua. We had nightly chats for the whole time he was away. He was always an outstanding signal; this was due to being very close to the sea, with a quarter wave vertical tank whip!

He wanted to operate more from home and decided to build a tower and install a two-element quad on top. He bought the box sections and had his friend who was an engineer weld the plates for the winch and pulleys. The idea was to pour a concrete block with a sleeve in the centre to remove the tower at a future date. Everything went fine with the tower and whilst waiting for the galvanising of the tower sections, Ron decided to pour the concrete. This is where he hit a major problem. Now please bear in mind that Ron is a very qualified electrical engineer and very intelligent man, but even clever people can have a "Grey haired moment."

To make the sleeve former for the tower socket, my friend decided to use wood wrapped in polythene and about three feet long. The idea was the wood would pull out because the polythene would act like a liner and slip out the concrete. Now me being clever (after the event) would have used a polystyrene former and when the concrete cured, I would have used a solvent to melt it away. Well poor Ron ended up in the "King Arthur Syndrome" i.e. sword in the stone, and no amount of pulling would release the former. The concrete had firmly gripped the liner and wood and no way was it going to let him get it out without a fight.

He cut the wood next to the ground and using a wood auger, bladed drill he set about boring holes into the top and scooping out the shavings which worked fine for the first five inches, but this was three feet long! Returning to his engineering friend, he had an extension rod welded which extended the auger by three feet, but this proved to be impossible to hold upright so he needed a step ladder to take on the task. The drill worked great, but there was a small problem of getting the shavings out the hole. Especially at three feet, He could only scoop out so much, but it being so deep proved impossible to get out the last foot or so.

Not to be outwitted he had a brainwave, pour petrol down the hole and light it. Down went the petrol and out went the flame. He forgot basic science from school; you need oxygen for a fire to burn, and being in confined space oxygen ran out quickly extinguishing the flame. Again thinking outside the box he decided to get air down the hole using a copper pipe and his wife's large insecticide pump, he pumped air under pressure down the hole. Well the result was spectacular. Vesuvius had nothing on it. The flames were about eight feet and burnt the shaving along with his eyebrows!

This left just about two or three inches of debris to be removed and the job would be complete. How do you remove the last of the debris? Again another grey haired moment, Out came his wife's cylinder vacuum cleaner! Down goes the tube and on with the switch, then all of a sudden a huge bang. The vacuum explodes expelling the motor across the garden and through the patio doors into the kitchen. Luckily the patio windows were open. The motor went off like a two bob rocket and was rodeoing around the floor! A quick dive at the plug switch brought the wayward motor to an end. As you can imagine, his wife was not impressed. So I am pleased to know that I am not the only Amateur enthusiast to have slight mishaps when installing our pride and joy.

*A little gaffer tape and it will be fine!*

## 9. Talking Stateside

One of my favourite things about Amateur Radio, is it plays to my strength. I have always been able to engage in conversation with people. This could be on the bus, train, or just in a queue. I think I am just one of those people that love to get to know people. My Mother always told me as a child I had been vaccinated with a gramophone needle! Now that is giving my age away, and for the people who do not know what I'm talking about check out Google. So, I think that it was a case of the Radio hobby finding me rather than me finding Radio.

I mentioned a little earlier that I have made a lot of friends in the hobby. Some of them have become very close to me over the years, and I have had the privilege to meet some of them. I will describe how I got on with them a little later, but I feel I must point out that I sort of got to know them over a long period, and not suddenly jumped in and invited them to become my best friend or potential son in law!! The thing I find funny when talking to someone on the radio is they never ever look how I imagine them to be. You only must go to a radio rally to see what I mean.

I have over the years been to many radio rallies, and I can certainly say that after the first one I quickly come to the conclusion that there are a lot of weird and funny looking people in this hobby! Now I'm not saying that these people are odd, but it's just as an observation. I mean I can hold my hand up and say I am ugly, in fact I probably abuse the word, but come on, I can't be the only person to have made this observation.

In fact I believe that the reason I do not dabble on amateur television is because I know I'm going to bump into some of these people. I don't believe there is a watershed on ATV!

This being said most people I have met have been really genuine and helpful, and I still maintain a lot of really good friendships over the years. Some breeze in and out of my log, and others I hear on a regular basis. Like Joe, WA2PJI. I first meet Joe when I was looking for American counties. Joe was from the Bronx, New York. We just sort of hit it off from the first QSO and it soon became a daily chat on different bands. Like a lucky pair of scoring underpants, I kept on or as near to a favourite frequency on each band, there was nothing magic about the frequency but it was just my spot where I'd done well calling CQ.

Joe and I met most mornings over the next few months. This was at a time when conditions were very good between England and North America. It was not unusual for me to put anywhere between four and six hundred entries a day. To help manage the qsl cards Joe offered to become my Stateside manager. This arrangement made it a lot less expensive as it meant Joe could purchase the cards directly saving me the price of shipping, plus the stronger pound meant the cards were a lot cheaper. Also it was cheaper to post from inside the states than for me to post airmail from here in the UK. This arrangement went on for the next twelve years.

In 1991 a friend of mine Ron G4DIY was going over to North America. He was going to see a mutual friend Dave KA2BOK whom had been over here a year or so earlier, Ron's itinerary was to see Dave, go to the ARRL headquarters, also to see New York. So I made up a parcel of gifts so Ron could pass them to Joe for me. When Ron got back home he told me of his adventure and mentioned that Joe was hoping that I would make the trip there soon. This was also mentioned by Joe during the course of our next QSO's. So I agreed that I would consider it for maybe the following year.

This was the best time to meet because Joe's young son was to celebrate his first communion, and on the 10th of May it was my birthday! Ron G4DIY would also meet up with me at the communion party and then a couple of days later we would all meet at the Rochester Ham- Fest. I also had made arrangements to go to the ARRL headquarters to get my DXCC and WAS (Worked All States) awards verified. I also planned to meet Ron AD4SZ in Kentucky. It was going to be a busy two weeks!

With everything sorted I was to meet Joe at JFK airport, spend two days with him in New York, then up to Newington CT to ARRL. Back to New York the next morning fly from LaGuardia airport to Charleston West Virginia and meet Ron, and his wife Thelma. Two days later back to New York collecting my hire car. Communion party that evening, then off to the Ham fest the following day. All planned and ready to go.

I was met by Joe at JFK, and taken to meet his family. Roe his wife had prepared a wonderful Italian pasta and real warm welcome. I had decided to stay in a small hotel nearby, but Joe insisted that I stay with his mother and father who lived close by. So. after our evening meal and an hour or so getting to know each other, I was taken to Joe's parents.

Joe's parents had emigrated in the early fifties to the United States from Italy, and Joe's father still had a very distinct Italian accent. I had no problems understanding him although both he and his wife spoke mainly in Italian when together. The next morning Joe's dad cooked a hearty bacon and egg breakfast, He told me Joe was just finishing some work and would be there shortly. Whilst sitting at the breakfast table Joe's father told me he worked for himself making ornate concrete blocks from various moulds for party walls, swimming pools etc., but was now semi-retired Plans made and finalised, it was agreed that I would travel to meet Joe in the second week of May 1992. I explained that I was a foster carer looking after young children. He was amazed that his son and I had met up via the radio and I think bemused that I had come to America to meet his son. What happened next was a little bizarre even for me. He pointed at the fruit bowl and picked up an apple. "This is what we call an apple." "Sorry" I said a little confused, he then reached to the bowl and picked out a Banana, "This is a Banana." Now I'm wondering if I have been left in the company of a madman, "ok" I said, as his hand is reaching for the next piece of fruit. I beat him to the pear and said "This is a pear, that's an orange and those are grapes" I picked up the fork and said "this is a fork" at that point I moved the knife, Just in case! "I come from Liverpool, not bloody Mars" I then beat a hasty retreat to the room I was staying in.

Joe arrived about ten minutes later and told me to get my cards ready for checking at the ARRL Headquarters in Connecticut. He told me that it would take about two hours to drive there. So, glad to leave my funny host, I got my DXCC and Worked all States QSL cards together and off we went.

I remember on the drive to Newington seeing large amounts of animals killed on the roadside. I saw deer, all types of birds, ground hogs and racoons. It really shocked me the amount of road kill and it surprised me no one removed them, some of which were huge.

*The stacked array waiting for us to play!*

On arriving at the ARRL I couldn't help but be impressed by the towers and mono band antennas stacked on them. On entering we were greeted by the receptionist. I was then introduced to Wayne Mills whom I'd met before at the RSGB HF Convention on a few occasions. If he didn't recognise me from Windsor, he sure didn't act like it. He greeted me like a long-lost friend. We dropped the cards off for checking, and Wayne showed me around the museum. I noticed in the reception area a qsl card from the infamous Romeo Stepanenko 3W3RR and

P5RS7. He had visited the ARRL just a week or so before me. I knew Ron G4DIY was coming to the Headquarters in the next few days, so I asked Wayne if I could post one or two of my qsl cards around for Ron to notice. Good enough he said yes, so off I went. Well I started in reception and the museum, toilets including the ladies just in case! Even in the card checking room and guest operating shacks. In fact, everywhere!

*Operating as W1AW*

I was invited to operate the club station as guest operator; I went on to 20 metres using a Kenwood and a kilowatt! Trust there to be a flare active as I got on air. So, I only worked a couple of local stations. Still I received my operating certificate for operating W1AW. So, with this and my other awards sorted we returned to Joe's QTH in time for our evening meal.

After our meal and an hour or so of talking and joking I telephoned Ron in Kentucky to arrange our meeting the following day. I was to leave in the morning for Charleston and I would meet Ron there for the drive to his QTH. During the conversation Ron asked me what I would like to eat. I explained I do not like spicy food, and I would not like to have possum nor grits! I don't know why I said this but I think it stemmed from the stories Ron told me about when we had our long talks on the radio. I recall him telling me he lived in "Hillbilly" Country and there were still a lot of mountain men where he lived. I'm of an age where I can still remember the Beverley Hillbilly's. So maybe that is what brought the thought to my head.

The flight from New York to Charleston passed very quickly. I was still overawed by the whole adventure. I found Ron with his wife Thelma in the arrival lounge and we put my luggage into his pickup truck alongside his huge dog called "Hound". Well that is what Thelma called it, Ron just called it "dog or Dawg" It was huge, some kind of Mongolian bloodhound or something. You know the type, a cross between a doormat and a bear! It was very, very, hairy and it really impressed me that Ron knew which end to feed or pat!

It was about a two-hour drive to Ron and Thelma's home in McCarr Pike County. We passed through some of the most spectacular countryside and mountains. The house was situated next to the Tug Fork River, and the bridge crossing took you into Matawan West Virginia. This was the town famous for the Hatfield and McCoy feud. It was also where Sid Hatfield shot the Felt detectives over the mining disputes in the early nineteen twenties'. In fact, Sid Hatfield is buried about one hundred metres behind Ron's house. History lesson over.

*Ron and myself at the Tug River on the Kentucky-West Virginia State line.*

We arrived at the house around four pm, and whilst Ron was showing me around his shack Thelma started cooking the evening meal. We were talking on 40 metres to a few of Ron's friends when Thelma announced dinner time. So, finishing the goodbyes on the radio we went to the dining room. Thelma brought over the plates and on it was what I could only describe as a rat in bread crumbs! I tried to not look shocked, but I don't think I got away with it. Passing other dishes with various vegetables on I tried to hide the thing under potatoes and beans. "Oh, like your vegetables then Lee?" Ron said, well like my Mother always told me "eat your vegetables first saviour the meat last." So, that was the tactic. But all I ended up with was the dead thing still there. Ron and Thelma had eaten most of their meal including the dead thing. Then it happened, both looked at me and Ron asked if there was something wrong with dinner. "Eh no I'm just following a home rule of eating the meat last" Looking down at it on the plate, it had little arms, and a little bigger legs, but most worrying was its head and very long tail!

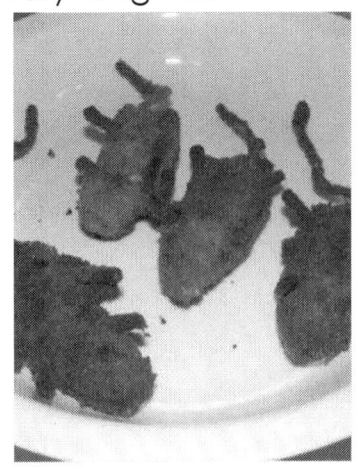

*Fried possum!*

I very carefully chose a tiny bit from the middle with my fork and then slowly placed it in my mouth. Still looking at me I then began to chew. Chicken! It tasted like chicken. Not as bad as I thought, then immediately they both burst out laughing. It was Chicken in bread crumbs. Thelma had shaped the chicken and coated it to look like a possum. "Possum is ok" said Ron, "but we prefer Chicken!" Even when they both came to stay with me here, I could never compete on the trick they pulled on me!

This chapter has been the most difficult to write. It was a little embarrassing for me to put pen to paper, as it shows me with that "Warts and all" kind of disclosure, but the kids insisted that I must share this moment with you the reader.

It was whilst I was visiting with Ron and Thelma in Kentucky. I wanted to have a little look around the area where they lived. As mentioned in an earlier chapter they lived in a really historic place. Across the Tug River, which is about eighty yards or so from their house, was the town of

Matawan. This small mining town was famous for the Hatfield and McCoy feud, and when in the nineteen twenties, Sid Hatfield shot dead a Felt detective. All this was on my door step so I decided to have a look around.

Ron had told me that he would take me into town later to have a look around, so I climbed up the hill immediately at the back of Ron's house to explore the cemetery. It was very well kept with most of the plots well maintained. I soon found Sid Hatfield's head stone which had been funded by the mining community for his sacrifice to the unions and local people. It was quite large in comparison with the other head stones.

*Sid Hatfield's grave*

Having taken some photographs, I went looking around at some of the other head stones. I noticed an area of the cemetery that was pretty over grown, so I decided to look over there. Walking through the undergrowth I made my way to a place that overlooked the river and town. Again a few photos' and then a slow walk back to Ron's home.

After lunch, as promised we went to Matawan for a look around. Matawan is steeped in history, and I would certainly recommend a visit there. From Matawan, Ron took me to visit with some of the other local Radio Amateurs in West Virginia. Where Ron lives, it is a dry county so no alcohol can be purchased there. After a few beers and good company, we set off back to Ron's house. It was on the journey back I started to get a really burning itch on my lower legs and ankles.

By the time I got to Ron's house it was really uncomfortable. I thought I must have either nettled myself or it was poison ivy rash, not that I have ever seen poison ivy! No. it was Chiggers! Both Ron and Thelma informed me. Now like me I bet your wondering what Chiggers are. Well I can tell you they are tiny little tick lava that eat you alive! Ron told me that they bury in and release some bug juice that dissolves your flesh and they feed of you eating you alive!

Not one to normally panic, now not wanting to be seen as a wimp, nor be eaten alive by flesh eating bugs, I calmly asked what the cure was. "Chiggerrid" said Ron, "but there is no pharmacy open now." With my legs on fire and itching I recall again calmly asking what we could do. "Amputation" Ron said, but out of the corner of my eye I could see Thelma in the kitchen laughing. Ron seeing how uncomfortable I was and told me not to worry it can be easily sorted. "We have no Chiggerrid at the moment, but we can use an alternative. Nail varnish!" Ron told me with Thelma nodding in agreement.

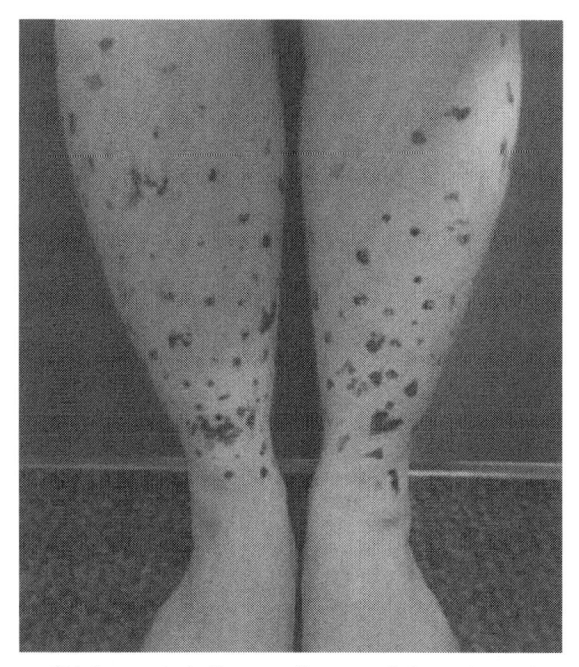

*Chigger bites all varnished up!*

Now I thought, as you are probably thinking. This is a 'wind up' and told Ron so. Ron telephoned two family members and asked them to confirm how to get rid of Chiggers. Both of them without hesitation said "Nail varnish." I felt at this point I had to believe him and to be honest at this point I didn't care as it was so painful. So out came the nail varnish and I was dotted and dabbed all over my legs where the bites were. I looked like Mr Blobby when they'd finished! How was I going to explain this to my wife when I got home? Ron took a few photos', and he gave me a copy to show Val when I got home, but I needn't have worried because it did not wash off for nearly a fortnight! It's a good job I am able to keep in touch with my feminine side! Even now the photograph is brought out at family or friends gatherings, and shown to everyone. I found out later nail varnish was an 'old wife's tale!' Antiseptic cream would have done it!

I was only in Kentucky for three days, and I have never met such hospitable people, I managed to buy my Kenwood TS440 and a Heathkit SB1000 linear amp. In one store, we went to the cashier told me I sounded just like John Lennon, she went on to ask if she gave me a book would I narrate it on a tape so she could just listen to my accent! So, I can now count myself as part of the fab five!

Returning to New York I collected my hire car and drove to Joe's house in time to meet up with Ron G4DIY and his friend John. We met at the school where the communion had taken place earlier, and where arrangements for the family party were to be held later that evening. Ron had not long arrived before me having returned from the ARRL Headquarters. He told me that he had seen my bloody QSL card everywhere, even in the toilet! I asked him if that elevated me to celebrity status, but he just told me to "Bog off!" I often wonder if that was because I'd left him my card in the Loo.

I went back to Joe's dad's house for a shower and change of clothes ready for the celebrations and when I got back I found a seat with Ron G4DIY. Joe had ordered in a barrel of Guinness believing that is what we drink here in Liverpool! And to be honest I do not drink that much at the best of times. Both Ron and his friend John were having a good time, so when in Rome! I think the fact that we where from England brought us to the attention of Joe's family and friends. Joe was a very good host introducing us to lots of people and in fairness he mingled well with everyone, but there is one introduction I recall most.

*Left to right myself, Joe's dad, his mum, and Joe.*

Ron, John and two other Amateur friends of Joe's and myself were sitting on some rather large barstools near to the bar. It was a couple of hours and a few beers into the party. Now I must stress that I did not have too many beers as I find Guinness a bit heavy in the stomach, but I don't need alcohol to make me talk, remember the gramophone needle thing mentioned earlier! Anyhow sitting near the bar Joe approached us with a work colleague. He told me she was his boss and wished to introduce her to us. It is at this point I would like to tell you that for some reason I have never be voted into the post of public relations in our local club! Despite nominating myself many times.

Joe started the introductions with Ron and ended with me. As I stated earlier I was definitely not intoxicated, maybe merry. I really am sorry but I do not recall the nice lady's name, but Sue seems to ring a bell. Anyhow Sue or Sarah asked how we met, so I explained through Amateur radio. I remember her being very attentive, and I recall Ron, John, and myself giving our accounts on who was who, and when. Sue asked me how I found America. So, I explained "I just got off the plane, and it was there" Now having experience with various North Americans on the radio I knew that most of our 'Off the cuff' jokes or sarcasm is wasted on them because although we share a similar language, it is not the same.

Here are some examples.
We call it a Bonnet they call it a hood, we call it the boot they call it a trunk, a bumper is a fender, wheel brace is a wheel lug, gear stick is a shift, windscreen is windshield and so on, and all that is just a car, by the way they call it a vehicle! Anyhow back to Sue or Sarah, I started asking her a few questions. For example, how long she had known Joe, etc I thought we were getting on really well, I asked were Joe fitted in at work and was he valued, I think when I asked her to give Joe a raise as he is so valued, things changed pretty fast. I noticed after Joe next got up after falling off the stool, taking her by the arm and quickly leading her away that it might have possibly been something someone said. I normally pride myself in

interpreting people's body language but I must have missed that one.

Well next morning I got up and had breakfast ready to go the hamfest at Rochester. Joe arrived with Roe and his son then we all set off around 7:30am.

I'd be telling lies if I said things were hunky dory, there was a bit of an atmosphere so I apologised for any embarrassment caused the night before, and blamed it on misinterpretation, language barriers, the Guinness and Ron. Anyway, Joe was very gracious in accepting my apology.

The drive to Rochester was incredible; the views along the way were fantastic. It was still hard to take in the amount of road kill there was, but hey it was just an observation. I passed through a lot of counties, some of which I still need. We finally pulled into Rochester in the late afternoon. The thing I remember most was all the flowering cherry trees lining the roads. It was like driving through pink snow!

We booked into the motel near the Ham fest and after a quick shower and meal we drove into the show ground. It was awesome! We got in about 4pm and only had about an hour before it closed for the day, but it gave me a chance to see a bit of the bring and buy stalls and whet my appetite for the next morning.

That evening we met up with Ron, John and Dave KA2BOK. Dave is a resident in Monroe, right near the Ham Fest. I had met Dave when he and Linda his wife came over to England a couple of years earlier. We all met at a western style bar! Now bearing in mind that I had upset my good friend the night before, I decided not to drink alcohol at all and stay safe with soda. (See I'm even starting to go native.)

Well I can honestly say I have never been in a bar like this in my life (and I've seen a few.) There were peanuts in barrels placed around; lots of shells were all over the floor. Just eat them and throw the shell away. The waitresses all wore gingham shirts, very short dresses, cowboy boots and hats! "Hi I'm Wendy and I'm yours for the night" Was the greeting I got when I sat down and was given a menu. The menu was like an old newspaper with the food (mainly steak) written in between Wanted posters! Well Wendy was gorgeous, and I remember saying "Wow! You'll do for me Wendy." When asked to place my order I asked for a "John Wayne Steak" she asked me what I meant, so I explained "One like John Wayne orders in the movies, you know about a foot long and about 2 inches thick and rare" off she went to the kitchen. About fifteen minutes later this slightly larger cow girl brought my steak out and informed me her name was Sue and that she was mine now for the night! When I saw this steak, I didn't know whether to eat it or climb it! Anyhow I knocked a big dent in it for England.

Now as it happens (I can't believe I wrote that!) Sue was very attentive and really charming. She enquired were we all family or friends? I explained that we were all Radio Amateurs and we were here for the radio rally at the Show grounds. She told me she had been serving some Germans yesterday who were also here for the ham fest. Sue asked where about did we come from, so I explained that Dave and Joe where from here in the States, but Ron, John and myself were from Liverpool in England. "Wow" said Sue "Do you know the Beatles?" I politely told her "No." I made a comment about the bar explaining how we did not have these kinds of western themed bars where I come from. "Oh" she said "Don't you have cowboys in Liverpool?" "Well Yes" I told her "We have window cleaner's, they're cowboys where I come from. In fact, we call our window cleaner Porthole Bill, because he never cleans the corners!" "Oh" She said "We have window cleaners here too as well as cowboys" then just walked off! I just looked at Ron and shook my head. Hoods bonnets, trunk boot need I say more? Roll on the peanut fight. England fought the lads from America, and I'm proud to say we won!

*Bottom Left to right Ron G4DIY, Dave KA2BOK. Joe jr. John G0LHN, and Joe WA2PJI. Top row Roe, (Joe's wife,) Linda (Dave's wife) and myself.*

## 10. Happy Harry

My introduction to Amateur Radio was very similar to a lot of other amateurs in the late seventies early eighties, CB. Yep, good old Citizen Band radio. In late 1979 I met a guy with a CB radio I was awestruck when he demonstrated a conversation with a gentleman in Kentucky. That was it! I wanted some of this.

At that time it was like joining a secret society, something on the lines of I know a man who knows a man who could possibly get his hands on a radio for you!

When I think back I believe it was like that because it was illegal to own or to transmit on eleven metres. You were classed as a pirate. Well what can I say but give me my radio, parrot, eye patch and bottle of rum. Yo ho ho. It's the pirate life for me.

It was not easy to get good advice or information about equipment etc. As people did not like to advertise the fact they were "on the air", But with aerials popping up all over place, it had to be one of the worst kept secrets I've ever heard of! I don't believe that the radio investigation dept needed much help finding offenders, and I firmly believe after witnessing some of the installations just locally that along with all the satellite dishes installed, it must have had a negative impact on getting planning permission for legitimate installations, myself included. I had an Avanti Moonraker IV at about forty feet, coupled to a Yaseu FT 707. My countries list rose very quickly, and I ended up with 216 countries worked and 175 confirmed. I was very serious about DXing.

It was early on a Friday morning when I got the dreaded knock on the door! The Post Office Radio Investigation Officer. I had been out the day earlier using my radio mobile, and as it was still inside the car, so I had no problem with his request to see my station. There was only the power supply there, and I was not one for displaying my QSL cards on the wall. I knew he did not buy into the statement that I had recently seen the errors of my way, and sold my transceiver, but he was really not such a bad guy. He told me he was passing when he saw the antenna. He told me he knew I'd been transmitting, and really would not like to come back to confiscate my equipment etc. So maybe If I were serious about radio then become an amateur.

The message was very clear, and I must admit by this time I really enjoyed radio, so I needed to join a group and study for the R.A.E.

So the decision was made to join. "A Proper CB club." It was there that I met likeminded people, the ones that were serious about DXing and not one of the "One nine a copy" group. Not that I criticised the idea of people making dates or whatever on their radio, but I believe the only thing that had "eye-balls" (high balls) were giraffe's! The group I joined had likeminded people who were in fact eleven metre pirates, the vast majority of which went on to help swell the ranks of Amateur Radio Op's.

There was a group of members that used the venue to ask questions and receive answers on the Radio Amateurs exam. Past exam papers were made available and Morse lessons were practised, members were all made welcome and invited to join in. Of course, the majority of members enjoyed just the social side of the club meetings but for me the opportunity was too good to pass. It was here at this club that I met my good friend and Mentor, Tony Bailey, G4XSN. He was the guy that taught me CW and is mentioned in other parts of this memoir. During December 1984 I took the R.A.E and in February 1985 got my B class licence G1MEF.

After becoming a ham, I continued to go to the old CB club to help out with teaching other members how to pass the R.A.E and some CW.

It was there that I met Bill. (later to become G0JID) His enthusiasm for radio was like mine, he had also worked a lot of stations and his country count was really high. He had taken his R.A.E in May and was waiting for his results. So whilst waiting he decided to learn CW. Bill had grand plans when he passed and we became good friends.

I recall the day Bills results came in. When he phoned me I remembered how excited he was, it was infectious Bill had been saving his money and he knew exactly what equipment he wanted. It was in fact Bill who asked me to help him install his tower and Arial mentioned in a previous chapter.

He asked if I would go with him to buy the radio on his next day off which was the Saturday. Bill had phoned the nearest shop to find out how much the guy would deal for cash on the equipment he wanted, and was disappointed with the offer, so he went to Stevens and James in Leigh near Manchester. Bill told me that he had made a really good deal with the owner Harry James, and believed it was because he was a Scouser (someone from Liverpool).

Saturday arrived and off we went, when we arrived at the shop we were amazed by the equipment on show. I noticed many QSL cards on the wall. One or two were from very exotic locations, one I recognised was from a location that I had worked the previous year. It was from OY Faeroes, and I noticed that Harry was one of the operators. Having sent for the card and not yet receiving it I started the conversation with Harry about working him and thanking him for the QSO. Harry told me he only sends out cards direct and if I wanted one I was to send a stamped addressed envelope to his QTH and I will get my card. When I asked if he had his log or cards in the shop he told me to "Sod off!!"

Bill then approached Harry and mentioned the phone call. He reminded Harry he wanted the Yaesu 757Gx the auto ATU, power supply and speaker I cannot remember the exact amount Bill put on the table in cash, but I do know he was saving about seventy pounds by buying it from Harry, than buying it from another shop in Earlestown.

Harry produced the items and asked Bill his name and address for the receipt. Bill told him, and then Harry wrote it down. Next Harry asked for Bills call sign. Bill explained that he had recently passed the R.A.E. and was awaiting his call sign to arrive. With that Harry ripped up the receipt and put the boxes under the counter "Come back when you have your call sign." To say we were gob smacked is an understatement, all that money on the table and he wouldn't sell! Bill and I went out of the shop. Bill was furious. Me, I just burst out laughing. Wow you have got to admire him giving up that large amount of money for a principle, although Bill didn't see it that way. So off we went to Earlestown, the owner had no such values and was happy to take Bill's money, including the extra seventy pounds! Bill eventually got his call sign, G0JID and as stated in another chapter we installed his tower and antenna.

The story of Harry doesn't end here. In years to come it would turn out that both Harry and my path would cross again, and we would become very good friends, but not to start with!

*Harry James G3MCN*

I duly sent to Harry a self-addressed envelope for my QSL card to get OY confirmed. About two weeks later the envelope dropped through the letterbox. When I opened it, there inside was my own QSL card, and written across the back was "Not in Log". I pride myself in the effort I put into getting into people's logs and I knew I had not made a busted call. I will not write here the names I called him, but I think I invented some just for him.

A couple of years went by and I was working a few VK-ZL on twenty metres SSB. I'd heard through the pileup ZK1. Now having worked several stations over the years it was the first time the Cook Islands had ever called me! "Go again please ZK1" I replied "ZK1XG" was the reply. "Hello Lee do I detect a Liverpool accent". He went on to tell me his name was Harry, he used to live in Liverpool and how pleased he was to contact me as he had not worked the UK since he arrived there a week earlier.

I knew exactly who he was and decided to get my own back "Hello Harry nice to meet you, I'm sorry to hear about the fire, by the way you're 5/8-5/9 here." After a short silence he asked what fire? I then said "You know at the shop." I could see his face and hear it in his voice "What Shop? My Shop? Has there been a fire in my shop? Has it all gone?"

"No I replied there was no fire but I bet you'll remember this QSO, and not put *not in log*' on this QSL card!"

I did not quite get what Harry said to me next, but after he said it, I did not hear him finish our QSO!

It must have been about six months later when I went the shop to purchase a mobile antenna, and I happened to mention the QSO, He threw me out the shop! My parting remark was, "Shall I send for the card direct Harry?" I'm sure he used the same words he'd used on twenty metres, although I might be mistaken!

From time to time I would hear Harry's signal on the air. Mainly 15 metres SSB. Harry lived on the ridge overlooking the Cheshire plains, near Delamere Forest.

Locally Harry was known for his sometimes-abrupt responses. His call sign was G3MCN and some said his call stood for 'Misery Comes Naturally', but I always thought Harry was not one to tolerate fools lightly. I admire his stance on principles and saw first-hand his integrity when he refused Bill the equipment he wasn't licensed for at that time despite all that cash on the table.

The Owl is OK | 111

Anyhow Harry sold up and retired to Delamere. He always had a big signal and never spent too much time getting into the DX logs. Then I didn't hear from him for some time.

It was only when he called me on fifteen metres one day I realised it had been quite some years since I last heard his station. He told me that he was on a dipole, and his tower and antenna where on the ground after a very bad storm.

For the next couple of months, he called to me and we had really good QSO's. I think back now and I believe the dipole was very low and poorly located and I was one of the only stations he could hear. During one QSO we spoke about his tower and I agreed that I would come to his QTH to access it and see if it could be reinstalled. Only on the condition that he would honour the ZK QSO with a card. I had plenty of cards from ZK but just thought I'd just throw that in.

I planned to meet Harry at his QTH, and I would assess the damage to his tower and antennas. It was tragic to see his tower lying in the undergrowth. It was fully extended and the remnants of a Hy-Gain four element twenty meter Yagi, plus a two element forty meter Yagi made by Mosley. The tower was a sixty-foot West tower and it had an electric motorised winch to raise the sections out. Harry explained to me that when the tower was originally installed it had tilted in a different direction, but because the trees had grown near to and around the tower, that so when it needed to be lowered it would not tilt over without hitting the branches of trees. Harry had asked another amateur for help and was told that the only way to fix the problem was to take the tower down and turn the base post by about forty degrees. I suggested to Harry it would be a lot easier if they had cut the trees back. Harry having mobility issues took the other amateur at his word and paid him to turn the base as suggested. The guy did this and everything was fine for the next year or so. That is until a very bad storm came in from the west which happened to be the most exposed side of Harry's location. That is when the tower went over. When I looked a little closer to see why the tower failed at the base, I was amazed and shocked to see the base was bolted to the concrete block with six two inch, yes two inch rawl bolts!!! The original 30mm bolts were still in situ and all the nuts had been put back on! I am amazed the tower up at 60 feet plus the twenty-feet stub mast with those two very large antennas on it stayed up at all. How it never ripped off the concrete when just lifting the tower and antennas vertical is nothing short of a miracle. I was unable to economically salvage the antennas, and because the tower had been lying down on a slope, both the rotator and winch had been exposed to the weather for about three years and were full of water.

I explained to Harry that the tower would be ok, but the cables, winches, rotator and antennas would need to be replaced. The base can be welded were it had broken the bolt down flanges, and it can be placed back on its original bolts, but the trees needed cutting back and some removed.

Now being honest, if this had happened to me at my QTH, I would find it extremely difficult to recover from this financially, Harry explained that when he retired he still had some stock, rotators antennas, coax etc. All he needed was a list of parts and the man power to do the project.

I asked a few friends that I knew to cut the trees down and clear back I managed to get Steve G0KXL to weld the new parts on the base, then we placed it back on the original bolts. The winches and new luffing cables arrived, Harry found a Yaesu GX 1000 in his garage along with a Mosley Pro-67 Yagi.

A week later we had it all installed, and Harry's call sign was once more heard in the pile up's, and I got my ZK1XG QSL card!!

*Harry's card, as promised.*

After helping Harry recover from his devastating loss, we become good friends. Over the years, I installed his various antennas, re-run coax and control cables, He gave me permission to shoot on his property. I took his QSL cards to the HF convention, and whilst there I had an opportunity to meet an old friend Ron Wills, ZL2TT, I have known Ron for a number of years, and worked him on many dx-perditions his most famous was from ZL8RI Kermadec Is, ZL7AA Chatham Is, etc and he was at the convention to give a talk on his latest adventure..

I met Ron as he was coming down the main stairwell at the Beaumont Centre Windsor; we went for a coffee and spent the best part of an hour getting to know each other. He was due to give the first of his talks on Kermadec, so we arranged to meet later.

After the DX dinner, Ron found me with a few friends near my favourite place, in the gardens outside. During the conversation, I was asked by Ron if I knew of any place he could stay as he had a further week to spend over here and he had not made plans. I explained that being a foster carer it would be impossible to offer my QTH, but leave it with me.

Harry was a bachelor of the old school, and he lived in a very large multi bed roomed dormer bungalow. When I phoned him he said "Yes" immediately. After the convention weekend, I met up with Ron at Harry's; Harry had arranged for Ron to give a talk on his adventures on Kermadec Island to the members of the Liverpool and District Radio Society.

I was really surprised when Ron opened up the talk by asking "How many people worked the station when they were on the island, apart from Harry and myself, not one of the sixty or so members got in the log, in fact I believe most members had never heard of Kermadec let alone know where it is! I guess not every ham is a "DX'er" or very good at geography.

Harry was never happy with the performance of his Mosley Pro- 67, and asked me to remove it off the tower and replace it with a Hy-gain TH-11. I took down the Pro- 67 and with help from my eldest son Lee built the TH-11. I was really impressed with the design of the TH-11 as it had no traps on the driven elements, which were full size, nor on the reflectors, they were full size on twenty and seventeen metres. It tuned up perfect and because of the log cell, it was very broad banded.

After installing the antenna, I took the instruction manual to the local post office and photo copied it!

When I got home I got the manual for my TH-6 out and checked the part numbers on the traps, they were the same! Happy days, I had a large collection of the aluminium tubing from other projects I'd built over the years, I also had various booms, so the only things needed were the insulators for the log cell, and u bolts along with channel the mount the elements onto the boom.

I approached Ron G1AOF (now M0COC.) Ron is a member of the same club I'm in, he also has access to a lathe at work, the tool needed to make the insulators for my project. Ron kindly obliged. The other things needed, were the boom to element brackets these were sorted by Steve G0KXL, again a fellow member or our club. Steve worked in a metal fabrication firm, and he made me twelve channels made of stainless steel! Each channel was eighteen inches long by two inches wide. They were never going to corrode. Last were the u bolts I needed for mounting the elements to the channel and the boom. These were provided by a local exhaust centre.

Over the course of the week I drilled the channels, mounted them on the boom, built the log cell and soldered all the pig tails, and assembled all the elements. I took down the TH-6 ready to install my homebrew eleven elements, five band Yagi.

Saturday morning I installed the antenna and fine-tuned it. The SWR was less than 1.2 to 3 across all 5 bands! So up it went to sixty feet and the first stations went quickly into the log. It was amazing; I had never operated on 12 or 18MHz before, and over the weekend I got over 120 countries worked on the two bands using SSB and CW.

It was about a fortnight later when I heard Harry. He was working North American stations contest style, one after another exchanging signal reports. As Harry was south of me and he was beaming northwest, the American stations were a lot stronger than me to Harry, in fact it was an

American who let Harry know I was calling him. I told Harry I was using a new antenna, and asked for a report as he was used to seeing my signal in the past. Harry stated I was an s point up to my normal signal. I deliberately avoided telling him at first the antenna I was using,

One of the Americans who had been listening on the frequency told us both that there seemed to be no difference in our signals when we were both beaming towards North America. It was then I told Harry about my new antenna. I would have loved to have seen the look on Harry's face when I told him that my homebrew TH-11 cost me the price of a couple of pints of beer, after he paid the best part £1200!

*Homebrew TH-11*

Over the course of the next few months Harry and I continued to compare signal reports and was always able to match his signal, until the day he bought his new linear.

Harry bought himself the Acom 2000A linear Amplifier; It was weeks before he told me how he had started to get an s point or two over my report. I bet Harry had wished he was in my shack when he told me! That is one serious piece of kit.

For years, I continued to repair and maintain Harry's aerials, his mobility was declining and it was becoming very hard for Harry to walk up his garden. The garden I might add comprised of a steep hill into which his house had been built on the lower third, the other two thirds where his tower was located was about nine hundred feet further uphill through what I could only describe as Bear Grylls country! Over grown wasn't the word to describe it. I'm convinced that had I looked around I would have met up with David Attenborough meeting up with a new unknown tribe of Cheshire pygmies.

Over the course of many years, Harry joined me on a few meet and greets, entertaining various Amateurs from around the world. They have of course been very memorable in their own right, but some more than others. For example, I used to be in regular contact on 15 metres with a gentleman of the cloth. He resided on a beautiful island in the central Pacific. I am not going to give his name here because I do not wish to cause any embarrassment to him. For a number of years, we would meet up and put the world to rights. His parents were both alive and living in Yorkshire. I had on many occasions telephoned them and passed over greetings, messages etc.

Then during one conversation he told me he was coming over to the UK to see his family, and he asked me if it was possible, he would like to thank me in person for making all the telephone calls for him. I don't know the exact words I said but I remember "yes" so long as he buys the first round!

I let Harry and a few of the other local Amateurs know and arrangements were made to meet at mine on the Friday he would be arriving. From there we would all go off to a nice pub nearby where I could claim my justly earned free pint, and they could all fend for themselves. Now it's at this point I feel I need to explain that the lads were meeting us here at 7pm but my friend (notice I haven't slipped up yet and revealed his name/ call sign?) arrived promptly as arranged at 5pm. The reason for this is because when my mother heard that someone off the radio I had been talking to was visiting me, she become very interested, even more so when I informed her he was a Jesuit Priest from an exotic Pacific Island. So she insisted I invite him to her house for dinner. My Mother being a good old left footer (Catholic) and my Dad an ex Orangeman, I tried to talk her out of her offer, boy did I try, but it was in vain. Not even the promise of free drinks in pub worked, so dinner it was. The only part of the argument I won that day was even though it was Friday "NO FISH"

I arrived at Lime Street Station five minutes early to ensure that I would not keep my guest waiting. It was then it dawned on me I did not know what he looked like. I must admit I was hoping he wouldn't turn up like brother Caedfeal!

I needn't have worried as I was able to spot him immediately! I noticed there was a definite lack of other passengers wearing a vivid yellow green, brown Hawaiian shirt, with matching khaki three quarter length shorts, finishing off with yellow flip flops. My friend had arrived.

With the usual introduction and greeting done we headed towards the car. On the way home I had this urge to tell him, no rather forewarn him about my parents, you know, get the apology in first. On arriving I couldn't help but notice the effort my Mum had put in. New table cloth, best dishes etc, you get the picture. Introductions made Mum sat us around the table and started to dish up the meal. She apologised for serving up meat instead of fish being it was a Friday, "It was out of my hands. These heathens out voted me" immediately Dad throws in "Don't worry about it Queen, where he comes from they probably don't have cows, I bet he's pissed off with fish anyway." Dad then starts tucking into his steak.

Then came the kick under the table, not even subtly, the mother of all kicks! "Ron," Mum said with a look that could cause the next ice age, "You forgot to say Grace" It is about now that I wish to be on that island my guest was from, I recall never, ever, ever tell my parents about visiting Amateurs, or at the least never let them meet. Thankfully my guest was very understanding although I think he was secretly enjoying my squirming and was looking forward to telling his parents and friends of the events that happened here.

Meal over I couldn't get out of the house quick enough. So off to my house to meet the lads and have that much-earned pint. We all went to the local and soon diplomatic relations between the church and the Pacific were restored.

Now there was a reason I have not named my guest nor given his call sign, it was after his third or fourth pint that he reached into his pocket and produced a certain banned herbal chill me out rollup. He lit it up and leaned back in his seat and exclaimed "Perfect end to a perfect day" Everyone at the table went quiet and just stared in disbelief, He then said "Sorry anyone want to share?"

I can still hear the laughter, and even now our friend in mentioned whenever we see each other. Harry was not impressed though and never spoke about it to me again.

Over the next few years Harry's health continued to deteriorate and he remained at home. His friends from the Chester Amateur Radio Club visited him regularly, and he was seen daily by his nephew Keith. Keith saw to his shopping and daily needs, but Harry was fiercely independent.

On Tuesday 9th September 2008 I received a telephone call from Keith to tell me Harry had passed away the morning before. He told me that it had been I believe an aneurism and it was while he was asleep. He went on to tell me he would let me know the date of his funeral.

It was about a week later that I received another telephone call from a gentleman named Dave. He informed me Harry was to be cremated and the service was at 12pm on the 18th of September, He then when on to tell me that he was the executor of Harry's will and I was a benefactor. To say that I was surprised and shocked is an understatement.

I went the service and meet with the family and friends of Harry. After the service, we went to a club in nearby Frodsham. I was approached by Dave and he told me Harry had left me his beloved Kenwood TS950, the Acom 2000a, tower and TH-11. I didn't know what to say. I was humbled.

## 11. Caravan and Other Sites

Back in the early nineties our club was donated a thirty-feet caravan to use as a shack. We had access to a farmer's field on top of Cleeves Hill at Aughton near the market town of Ormskirk. The site overlooked all of Merseyside and quite a bit of Lancashire. On a clear day, you could see right down the River Mersey as far as Frodsham, A large area of North Wales including the Great Orme at Llandudno and across Morecombe bay to the Lake District and Barrow-in- Furness. It was an HF and VHF operator's dream location.

Anyhow, back to the caravan. One of our members worked for the construction firm Search. He was given the caravan for the club and arranged for it to be transported to the farm on a low loader wagon. Getting it across the farmer's field proved to be a nightmare as the low loader could not get through the gate. So, we unloaded it into the farm yard. Paul G0JIB was the only member present who had a car with a tow bracket, so he was quickly volunteered in towing the caravan across the field. We then hitched the caravan to Paul's two litre Ford Capri and off we went.

Everything went well. Well almost! We got the caravan near to where it was to be set up permanently. This was to be under some trees next to a medium sized drainage pond. In order to get it in, we needed to jockey it a little bit to get it into position. I was placed at the front on the A frame where the tow hitch is located. Other members were placed at the rear. The idea was they would push and I would guide, good plan. We had just about got it in when the jockey wheel dropped into a rut in the field. John G4PKP who happened to be visiting us at the site to meet some members had got roped into helping us with our project.

He saw me struggle and ran to help me. He just got to my left side when suddenly the jockey wheel came free of the hole and the A frame swung to the left! I accidentally bumped into John knocking him down the embankment and into the pond! Now I call it a pond when in reality it was a large green slimy, mud filled hole surrounded by nettles and brambles.

John emerged like well I can describe as the legendry swamp monster! He was covered in green smelly mud, he looked like he had been dragged through a hedge backwards which in fact he had, but forwards! I would have extended my hand to help him back up the embankment, but as soon as I saw him emerging I couldn't stop laughing. Not my finest moment and thinking back I probably still wouldn't have held my hand to help, I doubt anyone would have. You could have caught anything! But I was really sorry.

*John emerging from the pond*

Thinking back, I don't think the fact that Reg G7DGH and Phil G4KIN helped matters by falling about laughing at the rear of the caravan. John just walked off. He never even said goodbye! I did not see or hear from John for many years, but gladly our paths crossed again more recently and our friendship is back on track.

As Kirkby, Amateur Radio club, we enjoyed the benefits the new shack brought us. We would meet on Wednesday evening and play radio, after wards we would then all leave and go for some refreshments at the local pub. We had quite a few special events at the site as well as some belting barbeques.

Sadly, over the course of a number of years our membership dwindled to just a few of us. We stopped doing very much at the site, and most of the meetings then turned to a social night rather than a club night. I think a lot of clubs suffered the same problems, no new members and a general lack of interest. Various theories have been put forward by lots of people, but I will not add to them.

I was a member of a contest group The South Wirral Contest Group. They in turn were members left from the old Elsmere and District Radio Club. I had over the years heard them on the air using their Club call and various contest calls. They were very active in the nineties and still meet to date. When I joined, I was never interested in contesting, but enjoyed the antenna building side of it.

They were quite a successful contest group winning plenty of different contests over the years. My part in the club was to build the antennas and install them on the towers we had. We had Yagis from 10 metres to 40metres. It was an impressive station.

Our site was from the back of a country pub in North Wales near the village of Holywell. The pub was called The Crooked Horn, and was located near the top of Halkyn Mountain. It overlooked Liverpool and was a vhf operator's paradise, but for HF being over limestone bedrock it had terrible capacitance to ground and proved later to be not so good on HF.

Over the years more and more houses were being built nearby, and we started to have breakthrough problems with the local residents. We only become aware of the problem when Alan the pub landlord told us the locals were not happy with seeing the antennas going up and we were causing television interference. To be honest this was the first time it had been mentioned to us. Alan asked us to find a new venue to operate from.

I approached the lads in the Kirkby Club and asked if they would mind us making use of the site at the farm near Ormskirk. As only five members remained in the club of which I was one, it was agreed to let the lads from the Wirral take over the site as long as they paid the farmer.

Many contests were entered and won from the site. The difference between this location and the one in Wales was like night and day. If we could hear them we got them in the log.

The site was really convenient for me as I lived about six miles from it, this allowed me to experiment with various antennas that I would like to try at home, without the inconvenience of taking my existing aerial down.

When we put the caravan in place, the farmer laid an underground armoured cable allowing electricity to the power points for the equipment. This allowed me to plug in power tools to help with my builds, and also for any work needed for repairs.

I had been given a 40metre two element beam from Harry G3MCN; it was badly damaged when his tower came down. Using bits of scrap aluminium tubing I was able to repair it. I knew that when it was fixed and installed, it would improve our competitive stance and hopefully our scores. At the site, we had two mobile lattice towers that can get the antennas up about seventy-five feet. So, we moved one into position and the lads started to bring the antenna across the field. The length of the elements was over forty feet and as they all lifted it the elements they encountered the electric fence! Whoever said you're never too old to break dance has never said a truer word. All four of the lads were jumping and screaming in unison. If you have ever seen the African tribe called Hottentots, well it was like the Scouse version of a dwarf Hottentot's synchronised formation team! They soon moved away from the fence, and to their credit they did not drop the antenna or damage it!

When it was installed onto the tower, it performed very well. It created a large pileup of Japanese stations just after sunset. I believe that is the first time none of the lads were in any rush to go to the pub!

*The 40 metre two element mono band Yagi*

I recall there being a group of lads going to the Spratly Island Group in South East Asia. I had managed to work them on all the higher frequency's, but near the end of their activity on the island I asked Steve

G0KXL if he fancied going up to the site to put up the 40-metre beam to see if we could get into the log on that band. Steve agreed and we met at the site about 4pm. It had been raining heavily for about a week, so hauling the tower out proved impossible. We just could not manually pull the tower as it sank in the ground; it was much too wet to get the car over to pull it out, so we just extended the out riggers out where it was, we then installed the antenna on it.

I recall the elements over the roof of the caravan, and when we fired up on 40 metres the lights all started to flicker. One of the biggest problems was the computer which due to the proximity of the antenna kept crashing. So back to pens and paper! We had it all ready to work the station, all we had to wait for was the band to open to the Far East and we should get into the log.

It was interesting on 40metres as the sunset, I called CQ and the first reply was a UA0 from Krasnoyarsk Siberia. This was then followed by a station from Indonesia. Steve and I both took turns at calling CQ, and we both worked several stations around South East Asia, including Japan. It was at this point I decided to have a look at the CW part of the band. I soon found the pile up and then I heard the station all our efforts were for, 9M0C. I split the VFO for about ten KHz higher and then called. To my surprise, he answered me first call! I looked at Steve and just smirked, Steve doesn't like CW and I could see the look of concern if 9M0C did not come onto SSB. I told him "There was no need to sit here listening for him to move to SSB, we may as well look to see if there is a station active there."

We made the move and almost immediately found the pile up on SSB. We listened to the station and where he was listening up on frequency, as I had worked them on CW, it was only fair to let Steve have the first crack on SSB. Again, first call Steve got in the log, so I then grabbed the mic and called, in effect tail ending him, again he come straight back. We were both amazed at how quickly we got into the 9M0C logs, and continued to get a few more into our logs before dismantling the antenna and putting everything away.

Without a doubt that antenna was a game changer, and allowed us to get very competitive scores in all our contests.

*Our club station antenna farm at the contest site.*

## 12. Family Matters

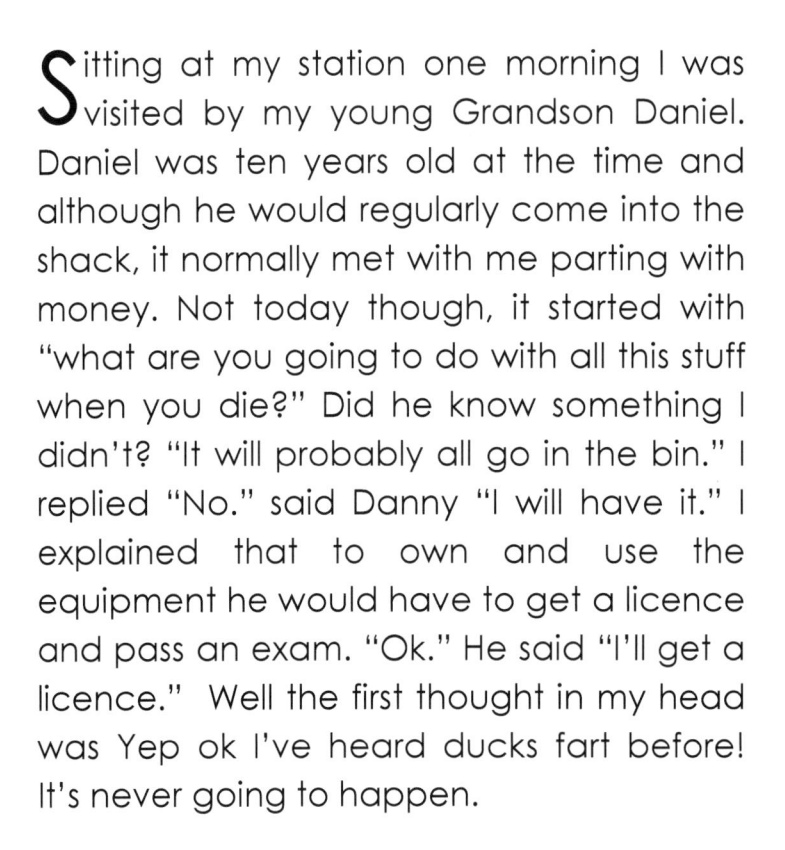

Sitting at my station one morning I was visited by my young Grandson Daniel. Daniel was ten years old at the time and although he would regularly come into the shack, it normally met with me parting with money. Not today though, it started with "what are you going to do with all this stuff when you die?" Did he know something I didn't? "It will probably all go in the bin." I replied "No." said Danny "I will have it." I explained that to own and use the equipment he would have to get a licence and pass an exam. "Ok." He said "I'll get a licence." Well the first thought in my head was Yep ok I've heard ducks fart before! It's never going to happen.

Several weeks passed, and I had forgotten the conversation. Then one day I mentioned to my wife there was a radio rally soon at Blackpool and I was going. Daniel was in the room at the time asked if he could go with me. I was really surprised at this because normally when I go to the rally my wife and the kids enjoy spending all my money in the town. "I could get my licence there." He said. I explained that he needed to study first and then take an exam. Not to mention I wasn't sure where he would be able to even go for the exam. I agreed that if he was serious about learning he would be welcome.

*"You want what when I die!"*

At Blackpool I met up with Dave and Cathy at the RSGB stand. I explained about Daniel wanting to become a radio amateur. They were both very supportive and told me about the training manual for the Foundation License. They were themselves facilitating the course at the Beacons near Frodsham. I bought the Foundation License book for Daniel. Dave informed me that they would be training next week, he told me to bring Daniel along and he could enrol with the view to take the exam over the weekend, sounds like a plan. On the night, I took Daniel to the Beacons, his sister Amy decided she wanted to join us. She decided she wanted to have her Foundation Licence too. Thirty-pounds lighter in my pocket I enrolled them on the course. It was to take place over the weekend with the exam on the Sunday.

I took them both on the Saturday and Sunday and at the end as promised they took the foundation licence. To my shock both children passed! Amy was nine years old and Daniel was ten. The first thing Amy said was "I've passed, great. What's the combination to the door lock?" It's hard to describe the feeling of pride I had when we got home and told the family, and the feeling of dread letting her loose on the world! I think in fairness Amy was the more confident of the two children, she quickly got into the swing of proper QSO's. She definitely wasn't a 5/9 person and defiantly had the gift of the gab! Poor Daniel was a little more mic shy and just a little wooden. It was like drawing teeth some times. I believe he was only in it for the equipment when I die!

One of the most memorable contacts I recall was when I was talking to a Saudi Arabian Station. It was in September 2005. I asked if he would like to say hello to Amy, a recently licensed YL. He agreed so I reduced the power to ten Watts to conform to her licence condition and off she went. Amy told Mohammed her name and QTH. Mohammed explained where he was and station details, Amy then told Mohammed what equipment she was using. Mohammed then asked if he could ask her a question, "How old are you?" he asked. Amy as quick as lightning replied "Really! It's not polite to ask a young lady her age, but on this occasion, I will tell you. I am nine years old." Well Mohammed was taken back by Amy's young age and told her he was very pleased to meet such an eloquent young lady! Amy on the next over asked Mohammed if he was Scottish! She told him "I'm looking on QRZ and see your wearing a dress! I thought only Scottish people wear a dress." Mohammed replied "No my dear, I am not a Scot and I am not wearing a dress. I am wearing a traditional Saudi dress because I am an Arab, not a Scot." "Well" said Amy, "How can you wear a dress that isn't a dress? Weird thing this amateur radio! Mohammed burst out laughing and later went on to send Amy a card direct.

*"Are you a Scot?"*

Both Amy and Daniel followed in my footsteps of chasing countries. I thought sending my cards was expensive, everyone was sending their card direct and it was costing me a fortune! Amy racked in a few more countries than Dan, she was very active and in all honesty like a breath of fresh air. People where very keen to talk to her and like every young woman she enjoyed the attention she got. Things were going well, I got an opportunity to get on the radio when the kids were in school or went to bed!

In October 2005, Ron G4DIY went over to the Isle of Man. I was checking around on 17 metres when I came across him. I called Daniel who was home for his dinner to try and get Ron in Daniel's log for a 'new one.' Daniel called for about twenty minutes but could not break Ron's pile up. So, I got on the mic turned the linear on and with 400 Watts I managed to break through. I asked him to listen for the low power station calling him, Ron then asked the pile up to stand by. Daniel called him using ten Watts and Ron didn't get the full call, Ron struggled with Daniel's call but after two or three minutes Ron managed to pull him in. I then tuned up the drive and put the linear on and thanked Ron for his help.

*Daniel trying to call Ron on the Isle of Man.*

Although Ron gave Daniel a 3/3 report. Daniel was made up. For the record, Ron gave me a 5/8.

Glancing at the DX cluster, I then noticed an announcement stating 'M3JIH 10Watts my arse! Who the F*** are they kidding.' Danny who was only 11 at the time was confused and understandably upset that someone was swearing about him. I told him not to worry and I shipped him back off to school. It was clear the author's call sign used to make that un-solicitored remark was one I recognised, and to say I was upset was an understatement.

Although I knew the call sign that had been used to send the announcement, I would never have guessed the guy would be stupid enough to either announce it or author it with his call sign. So, I telephoned the sysop of the cluster and enquired about the remarks on his system. He informed me that a certain station had logged off the system, logged in using the offending call sign. After the remark was put on the cluster, he then logged off and re-logged back on with his own call sign. The sysop remarked that all the connections were all from the same IP address and he went on to tell me who the person was.

It turned out I knew the offending author very well, he had always come across as a friend. It was well known he had a prejudice against foundation licensees.

Because of his actions he effectively put both children off air. He continued to deny his actions when I confronted him so leaving me no other option than to report him to Of Com. It ended with the guy getting a formal reprimand. I saw him once at Blackpool radio rally and pointed him out to Daniel. I told Daniel "I will show you where he lives when your 18." I must admit I never did. Amazing the things, you say in the heat of the moment. Last year I was at another Radio Rally when I was approached by, I am trying to think of a word to describe him but I am really struggling, anyhow he told me a long time had passed and we should put it all behind us. Thing is he still denies he did it even though it was proven by Of Com and more importantly he has never apologised to Daniel. I just left him standing there like the sad old man he is. Needless to say, he made it onto Lee's List of Dick heads!

I have over the years heard on the air many strange conversations, comments and statements that have been worthy of being entered onto my List of Dickheads. This list is kept near to the radio where of course when I hear a comment of worthy note I add the name to the list and give it a star! For example, I heard a station talking to another about aerials. This immediately drew my attention. He was explaining to another station how to build a quarter wave vertical. He informed his friend "To build the vertical you need a piece of copper pipe, then you cut a foot off it!" there was no mention of the starting length of pipe to start with. I mean what if the pipe was only six inches long? There was a certain Sicilian amateur that caused lots of problems on twenty metres. He got a couple of stars with some of the remarks he came out with.

As I stated earlier the list was kept on the wall near to the radio, and on one occasion I had an unannounced visit from a local amateur who was on the list! In fact, I believe he had two or three stars credited to him. I must admit I was a little embarrassed when he saw it and I have never heard a person plead his case for not getting on the list in the first place, and then try so hard to get off it! Well that certainly warranted another star!! (He is by the way still on it!)

I could certainly write many more chapters in this book on my involvement with amateur radio. For the most it has been very positive. There are times when I wish I had never heard of the hobby. For example, the time when the children got put off by a narrow minded bigot, but I think the worst time ever was when my wife was really badly injured whilst helping me, and to this day I still wonder why I am in this hobby.

I was installing a five-element beam for twenty metres. The tower when it tilts over takes the antenna over the fence into my neighbour's garden. So any work on the antenna has to be done from his property. I have a really good relationship with my next-door neighbour and it has nothing to do with me being an ex-heavyweight boxer!

I had tilted the tower over with the help of Val, my wife. I had just finished installing the reflector element onto the boom when I asked her to start to wind the tower up just a bit until I got around to my back garden. Val took the tower up about two feet; I was under the boom looking to see if the elements were in alignment when the tower suddenly dropped. I dived out the way but the antenna hit a tree and bent both the reflector and driven elements.

The stub mass crashed onto the top of the fence which prevented the tower hitting the floor. I heard a yell from my wife's direction and thought at first it was a warning from Val because the winch had slipped, it turned out it wasn't a warning, it was a cry of pain. The winch was not an automatic braked winch with a friction plate, but just a ratchet type with a simple lever which as the handle slipped from Val's hand started to spin extremely fast as the tower dropped towards the fence.

Val tried to stop the winch by making a grab for the handle, and before she knew it the handle hit her hand and fingers about three times as it was spinning so fast. The spinning handle broke three of Val's fingers in three different places; it also hit her wedding ring and squashed it almost flat. Which we later found out had shattered the bone. I ran to the kitchen grabbed a wet tea towel and wrapped it around her hand to try and prevent swelling and slow the bleeding.

I immediately took Val to the local A&E where she had her wedding ring cut off and a lot of X-rays. The X- rays showed Val had three fingers broken, seven of the joints where the fingers met were broken, and the bone that her ring had been on had splintered. So, after twelve stitches, and a temporary cast, and four hours in hospital she was allowed home with an appointment to see the orthopaedic surgeon the following day.

I thought it only fair to cook the evening meal.

Next day I took Val to her appointment at the hospital, the doctor examined her X-rays and commented on how badly her fingers were broken. He explained that her hand needed to go into a traction device to help the bones heal straight and even with this treatment he wouldn't rule out surgery. I really did feel bad; I had never given it a thought that an un-braked winch could do so much damage.

Eventually after six weeks in traction, Val's hand could come out of the cast, but it took months of physiotherapy before her hand was any where near healed, even now she suffers with pain in it.

I purchased new winches with the auto braking system soon after the accident, and managed to get the antenna up on the tower. I really cannot emphasise the importance of safety when working on Towers, or installing antennas. So, if like me you hate doing dishes (I had to do them for over six weeks.) heed my warning and ensure you have auto brake winch.

## 13. The Channel Islands

Back in the early 2000's, I was asked to join Ron G4DIY on a club DX-perdition to Guernsey. The usual partner who accompanied him had to pull out. Ron had made regular trips to Jersey and Guernsey, but he needed a replacement. I was both honoured and pleased that Ron chose me as there are several really good operators locally he could have of chose from. I recall the first time we went to Guernsey which was an incredible experience. To be honest I really did not have a lot of confidence in the vertical antenna that Ron had told me we would be using, and thought it would be more of a leisurely experience and very laid back. Just like a holiday.

I could not have been more wrong. We operated from the rear seat of Ron's Peugeot Estate car. Ron had really thought things through and we were a portable station, definitely not mobile. We were using all of Ron's equipment as this had been all tried and tested by Ron and his previous companion. I was aware I had hard shoes to fill, as John was an excellent operator and the logs were testament to this.

*Operating at the back of the car.*

You need to see this setup when it is completed state; it's really a fully functional HF station, one that you would be pleased to have at your house. It consists of Ron's ICOM 756 Pro II. The Dentron MLA 2500A Linear, the paddle/memory unit is home brew built by Ron. The computer when I first saw it resembled an Abacus! It looked so old. It was a Toshiba Satellite 256 using DOS! I asked Ron "Why is it so old? I mean using DOS!" I then offered the use of my all singing laptop from home. Chuckling Ron explained to me that the computer was bomb proof, but more importantly DOS takes less than a minute to load, were as windows is extremely slow in a pile-up. Looking back, we have in all the years' operating in GU – GJ only had to restart the PC once, and this was only because I had forgot to plug in the power supply and the battery died!

The antenna of choice is a vertical; the aluminium tubes of which there are seven are roughly three feet in length and they fit inside each other. So it easily extends to thirty three feet for forty metres, and telescopes in for the other higher frequencies up to ten metres. It is secured to the generator. The ground system consists of about one hundred and fifty to two hundred and twenty radials, all of which are non-resonant as this would detune the antenna as they are lying on the ground. The amount has over the years caused many a debate and discussion, both on and off air. They lower the angle of radiation and give the antenna something to work against.

*Ron G4DIY and my-self G0DBE antenna and radials.*

On each trip, we talk to between four thousand and five thousand other Radio Amateurs, and anywhere between one hundred and ten to one hundred and fifty countries over the four days we operate. Of course, that is depending on propagation. So, when you work out we normally get on the air at about 9am until 9pm. I think we do rather well. Ron would work until the pile ups die, but me; I'm like Cinderella, always in bed before midnight!

I like Jersey, but really prefer Guernsey, whilst in Jersey we met up with Craig MJ/K3PLV, and Peter MJ/K8PJ. They had both come over from North America to Jersey every year to guest operate the radio station. I recall whilst we were operating from Saint Ouens Bay we were into a major JA pile up and the lads from America were operating from Jersey Radio Club. They heard us working JA, but they could not hear the pile up! They travelled in their car to where we were operating on top of an old-world war two gun emplacement. I think it's fair to say they were surprised and suitably impressed with the station set up. Later I went for a meal with them both; Ron wouldn't leave the pile up! It was there that Craig told me the he had thought we were "Winding him up," when he heard Ron working the Japanese Stations. He told me they could hear Ron fine but not who he was talking to. He explained that even with the clubs three element beam they could not hear the stations through the high noise level! What could I say to that?

Myself I preferred Guernsey, I enjoyed Jersey but I talked Ron into going to Guernsey. I think this is because it was a little less expensive as we did not need to hire a car to get back to the hotel. Also, we were not as isolated where we set up, it was a car park and lots of people come to see what we were up to. We set up at Cobo Bay, which was only about half a mile from the hotel. Very convenient for both food and the Loo!

It was on our second day at the car park, when we met up with the local council workers. They were there on the beach to remove a dead pig which had washed up. They explained that they had seen the radial system on the bank next to the car park and were going to clear it away after collecting the pig off the beach believing someone had dumped them. I explained that we had left them over night to help us get on the air next morning quicker. The council workers were fascinated by the whole set up, and returned at dinner time to see who we were talking to as they ate their carry out lunch. As Ron was in the middle of a pile up, and seeing them tucking into their lunch, I realised how hungry I was, so I asked the driver to nip down to the local fish and chip shop and get some fish and chips for Ron and I, which he kindly did. (I did offer to let him keep the change!) Ron was sort of taken back at me being so forward with them, but never the less he enjoyed his dinner.

*Norman, and Tom, the lads from the council.*

Over the years, we have had a vast amount of people come to visit us, and during the time when I was not operating, I have been able to wind a few of them up! It can really wear you out when you are continually asked what it is you are doing. Ninety-nine times out a hundred I'm a good advocate for the hobby, I explain that we are Radio Amateurs from the mainland there to help fellow amateur enthusiasts from all over the world have an opportunity to talk to likeminded people from the Island of Guernsey. Unfortunately, after about thirty or so on the third day it asking the same questions it can be a bit repetitive. So, when this couple asked me what we were doing, I replied "We are with the BBC and because of the number of complaints about bad reception during the cricket, we are here to help boost the signal around the island." On the last day (Monday) the same man approached us and told me "You are doing a sterling job and the cricket program has never been so clear!" Wow! So, once I got away with this wind up, I just had to see what else I could get away with.

Now I know a lot of people think that I am casting a bad light on the hobby, and missing a golden opportunity to show Amateur Radio in a positive way, but I just couldn't help it! It just sorts of pops out before I realize that I have said it. For example, I was sitting in the car park whilst Ron was back at the hotel having his lunch; I was approached by a lady who boldly knocked on the window of the car. Bearing in mind I was in the middle of a big pile up of Stateside stations and she was about the tenth person that morning to ask, no demand, to know what I was up to. Without a second thought it just popped out, "Spies", she just slammed the door and left me to the pile up. About fifteen minutes later Ron arrived and I handed over the pileup and off I went for lunch.

When I came back about three quarter of an hour later, I found Ron outside the car in the company of the local police. At this stage, Ron was showing them our past QSL cards and going through different equipment in the station (car). As I arrived Ron gave me a very nasty look and told them I was the culprit. It turns out the old lady got home and dialled 999 and told the police that spies were in Cobo Bay car park and they were passing information on God knows what, and to get there as soon as possible. Of course Ron, who had been left on the radio had to explain what we were doing, and after showing our radio licenses and some cards plus a small demonstration on the radio they were suitably satisfied that we were not spies, and warned us in the future not to tell the local member of the Women's Institute otherwise. Point taken, No more spies!

On another occasion, again after about the third day of explaining to locals what we are doing, I informed one enquirer that we were seismologists. We were there to measure the impact of a possible tsunami on the Channel Islands should the cliff face on one of the Canary Islands slip into the sea. Seeing all the radials on the ground of the base of the antenna, and the computer with all the call signs and reports, he bit hook line and sinker, but I did not expect the next thing he said. "Typical, I'm a member of the parish council and they never tell me anything" with that he stormed off. I looked at Ron who just shook his head and told me if the police come this time I have got to deal with them. They never came nor did we see the guy again.

Over the years, we have been visiting the island my explanations for what we are doing there have ranged from global warming, submarine monitoring, communication relay for SETI (search for extra-terrestrial intelligence), Survey for an offshore wind farm. That one didn't go down well. One that nearly got me lynched was when I told a couple of dog walkers that we were doing a feasibility survey for fracking!

There was one occasion when we had four days of intense pileups. Ron had gone for lunch and I was really exhausted. I told the pileup I was just going to refuel the generator. As a ploy, just to get a drink and a two-minute break. Ron was gone a little longer than normal and my ears were sweating from the headphones. I was leaning forward on the front shelf, when the door opened and two lovely old ladies asked if I was ok. Then it just popped out. I was tired and diabetic, hungry and my friend was late coming back to give me a break.

About fifteen minutes later they returned with some lovely cakes and a flask of coffee. Just then Ron came back, and the two women started telling Ron off for leaving me and telling him that he should know better. Ron just stood there with his mouth open and the women stormed off. I then offered Ron a piece of cake. That didn't go down well, but the cake did.

I mentioned in previous pages about the bin men (the refuse collectors) Norman was the driver; Tom and Alan were the other crew members. During the course of the last eight or nine years we have been going to the island, we have been visited by the lads on many occasions. They know roughly when we will be visiting Guernsey, and they then keep watch for the antenna or the radials which we leave over night to save time the next day. They then spend some time with us whilst they are eating lunch.

I have been asked on many occasions what Guernsey is like, and to be honest I don't know. I must explain I have only seen St Peter Port, the road which takes us to the hotel and the car park! So, when the lads from the council asked if I would like to accompany them for an hour or so, I was off! I put on Alan's high viz jacket and hat and waved to Ron as we drove off in the wagon! Ron who was on the air at the time just stopped speaking on the radio his face was a picture! Leaving Alan with Ron, off I went.

We collected a mattress which had been fly tipped then Norman showed me around the island, what a beautiful place. After going around the island it was then when I decided if I were to move to Guernsey, then I would change my job to a glazer. I have never seen so many greenhouses! I would never be short of customers and from the safety of the road or field with a catapult and stones I would be guaranteed work (I feel at this point I must explain I am only joking. Just in case some greenhouses over there have had unexplainable breakages.)

Sadly, on the last two trips the lads have not been there to visit us. I later found out from Norman who was passing the car park with his wife and saw the antenna then called in to see us. He told us Tom had been going to the mainland for radium treatment, Norman had retired, and Alan made redundant, to us it was the end of an era.

## 14. For Ron, Alan & Lee Junior

For many years now I have accompanied Ron on many of our expeditions to Guernsey, but in 2013 I developed a problem which left me unable to go with Ron. He postponed the trip and we rearranged from the October to March which is when we normally went. Again, due to ill health I had to let Ron down, I needed a replacement for me and I approached Alan G4NXG.

*Alan G4NXG*

Alan is well known in the DX world for his mobile work to which he has reached the top by attaining DXCC#1 Honour roll. His personality and all round operating skills meant he was the perfect choice for helping Ron. At first Alan was resistant believing he might let Ron down, but I knew from experience he was the ideal partner to go with him. In March 2014 Alan and Ron went over to the island, and as I thought they made a really good team.

Alan really bailed me out by helping Ron and I am very grateful. In the October I went again with Ron but I knew I would be unable to lift the generator and set up the antenna side of the station whilst Ron set up the station. So I took my son Lee jnr. He is not interested in amateur radio, but he has helped me no end in antenna projects and setting up. He is very intelligent and strong so lifting things were no problem for him. I was unable to get my wheelchair over to the hotel so it meant using crutches, by the time I got to the hotel I was too exhausted to get back to the station so it meant leaving Ron with Lee Jnr for company to carry on.

Lee did a fantastic job in setting the antenna for each band, setting up radial and taking it apart of a night when finishing for the day and next morning setting it all up again. He was a real asset. On the way home Ron could only sing praises for Lee which made me really proud. I discussed with Ron the prospect of Alan G4NXG accompanying Ron in the March 2014 and I would go with Lee again in the October 2014 this had worked out really well. Alan went in the March for the second time and I went with Ron and Lee in the October.

It was on this last trip I think I realised that it was getting too hard to get around, and I was relying on both Ron, Alan and my son Lee to do all the work. I feel now the time is right for me to stand down as Ron's companion, and let Alan take my place permanently.

I have a lot of very good memories from my adventures with Ron on our activity from the Channel Islands; I have met a lot of interesting people, and made some really good friends. I cannot thank Alan enough for all his help; also it would be remiss of me not to thank my son Lee for being there even though he does not have an interest in talking "on the air."

## 15. Reflections

There have been times over the years when I look back and reflect on my life since embarking in the hobby of Amateur Radio and I think actually believe that what started off as a hobby has ended up as a way of life. When I talk to other likeminded people about their experiences in the hobby, I find that although we have something in common, we all get something different from it. I cannot speak for others, but I firmly believe that life for me would not have been half as interesting if I had not stumbled over that gentleman on eleven metres all those years ago. You are probably wondering why I have wrote this all down, when you yourself have had as much out of the hobby as I have, but the truth is when I talk to my other Amateur friends, they do not seem to have had an varied experience as mine. It was my daughter and sons who asked me to write this record of my involvement in this hobby. For those of you who may think that what I have written is a work of fiction, then I can only tell you is that you're wrong. I have only written a true account of my involvement and exploits in this incredible pastime.

*The owl was OK though!*

## Glossary

***DX*** - Long distance radio communications, often from one continent to another.

***Call Sign*** - The grouping of letters and numbers which uniquely identifies a radio amateur eg G1MEF.

***JA/VK/ZL*** - DX call signs (from the UK), Japan, Australia and New Zealand

***Morse Code*** - The telegraphy code invented by Samuel Morse.

***CW*** - Carrier wave, often used to denote the method of radio communication using Morse code.

***CQ*** - The shorthand letters used in both morse code and voice radio communications; it means 'Listen to me, I'm calling out to anyone who is listening and wants to chat'. Two letters is certainly better than that mouthful isn't it?

***QTH*** - Location, whether in the home radio shack, on the road or on top of some mountain.

***/P*** - portable radio operating, in the great outdoors whether it's on a beach or on top of a Welsh mountain.

**/M** - mobile radio operation, usually based in a motor car but it could be a motor cycle or a pedal cycle.

**HF** - High Frequency, from around 1 MHz to 30 MHz, where MHz stands for million cycles per second.

**VHF** - Very High Frequency, from around 30 MHz to ??? MHz.

**UHF** - Ultra High Frequency, from around ??? MHz to ??? GHz, where GHz stands for a thousand million cycles per second - some number eh?

**PL259** - A commonly used plug or socket on the end of coaxial radio leads.

**Linear** - An amplifier which takes a signal input at one end, at say 10 watts, and outputs it at the other end at around 100 watts (ie an amplifier gain of x10) without, and this is the important thing, any noticeable distortion - in other words in a linear fashion.

**ATU** - Antenna tuner unit, is a device connected between a radio transmitter or receiver to ensure the power transfer between them by matching the impedance of the radio (50 Ohms) and or feed line to the Aerial.

***Rotator*** - a motor attached to an aerial which turns the aerial in the direction you want the strongest part of your radio signal to go. You only use a rotator if you've got a directional aerial.

***QRP*** - this is where a radio operator uses extremely low output power from his transmitter, which can be from around 5 watts down to thousandths or millionths of a watt ie mW or µW.

***QSB*** - Fading of a radio signal.

***XYL*** - Radio ham slang for wife or loved one.

***Harmonics*** - when transmitting a radio signal at the fundamental frequency it is most important that the harmonic frequencies (1st, 2nd and 3rd from the fundamental) are much reduced compared to the fundamental. They will always be there but shouldn't be strong enough to interfere with other equipment nearby - especially neighbour's televisions!

***73*** - means best wishes, it is normally only used when using Morse code, but has regularly been used by ssb operators.

Printed in Great Britain
by Amazon